Doing Sociolegal Research in Design Mode

I0129071

This book is the first to explore what design can do for sociolegal research.

It argues that designerly ways—mindsets that are practical, critical and imaginative, experimental processes and visible and tangible communication strategies—can be combined to generate potentially enabling ecosystems, and that within these ecosystems the abilities of a researcher to make meaningful contributions and engage in meaningful research relations, both within our research community and in the wider world, can be enhanced. It is grounded in richly illustrated examples of sociolegal researchers working in design mode, including original individual and collaborative experiments involving a total of over 200 researchers and experts from subfields such as social design, policy design and speculative design working on issues of sociolegal concern. It closes with an opening—a set of accessible sociolegal design briefs on which the impatient can make an immediate start.

Written by an experienced sociolegal researcher with formal training in graphic design, the book is primarily focused on what the sociolegal research community can take from design, but it also offers lessons to designers, especially those who work with law.

Amanda Perry-Kessaris is Professor of Law at the University of Kent.

Doing Sociolegal Research in Design Mode

Amanda Perry-Kessaris

Routledge
Taylor & Francis Group

LONDON AND NEW YORK

First published 2021
by Routledge
2 Park Square, Milton Park, Abingdon, Oxon OX14 4RN

and by Routledge
605 Third Avenue, New York, NY 10158

Routledge is an imprint of the Taylor & Francis Group, an informa business

© 2021 Amanda Perry-Kessaris

British Library Cataloguing-in-Publication Data
A catalogue record for this book is available from the British Library

Library of Congress Cataloging-in-Publication Data
A catalog record has been requested for this book

ISBN: 9780367177652 (hbk)
ISBN: 9781032131702 (pbk)
ISBN: 9780367177683 (ebk)

DOI: 10.4324/9780367177683

Typeset in Times New Roman
by Deanta Global Publishing Services, Chennai, India

For Chandra Lekha Sriram. Hah. x

Contents

Acknowledgments

'I can see the potential of design as a mechanism to give some structure to the process of project development and delivery but the chapter you sent doesn't whet my appetite.' So read one of the earliest comments on a draft chapter. Thank you for testing out my early and late drafts and reporting back honestly Emily Allbon, Davina Cooper, Ruth Dukes, Fleur Johns, Lucy Kimbell, Antonia Layard, Ramia Mazé, Grainne McKeever, Les Moran, Deger Ozkaramanli, Flora Renz, Steven Vaughan, Dawn Watkins and Clare Williams.

Thank you to the critical sociolegal community at Kent Law School; and for financial support from a Socio-Legal Studies Association field work grant and a Leverhulme Trust Research Fellowship (RF-2019-045). I want here to commemorate the fact that at the very time when I benefitted most from this support, the everyday hopes and dreams of so many millions have been rendered temporarily or permanently impossible; and to thank those researchers from other disciplines who have dropped their personal projects to focus on tracking and tackling the pandemic.

For your time, generosity of spirit and leaps of faith, thanks to all those whose collaboration and participation in experimental activities has generated much of the evidence base for this research—especially the students, it is a great privilege to travel with you as you create new spaces. And thanks to Tony Pritchard and Paul Bailey at London College of Communication for their teaching, which has transformed mine. For kindly granting permission for your work to be reproduced, and for supplying essential contextual information, thank you Jessie Sandhar and Geoffrey Omony, Danish Sheikh and Andre Dao, Jack Tan and Lizzie Coombes, Forensic Architecture, Sarah Browne and Jessie Jones, Joanna Perry and CEJI.

Who and where would I be but for friends and family? Thanks to my parents for being forever curious and interdisciplinarian; to my children for the special delight of working through some parts of this book with each of you in Cyprus; and to Jo for all the coffee-laced soothing and strategizing.

Goodbye, dear George. When I am next able swim in your sea I shall think of your tales of a Kyrenian childhood, especially the glass fish viewer, the borrowed fruit and the pet bird. And Nicos, how is it that you always know which is the book for me, my love?

Amanda Perry-Kessaris
April 2021
London

1 Towards a proposition

I am going to do what I can to show you how I arrived at this opinion … I am going to develop in your presence as fully and freely as I can the train of thought which led me to think this.

(Virginia Woolf)

This book explores the proposition that sociolegal researchers can and ought to draw on design to enhance their ability to understand and meet the methodological challenges they face.

Design is a varied and shifting field of practice and scholarship which, like sociolegal research, resists precise definition. When I use the term 'design' I mean the planning and making by humans of tangibles and intangibles including images, objects, places, activities, policies and systems. Designing is a core human activity—we all do it every day (Simon [1969] 1996, 111). However, I will reserve the term 'designer' for those who have 'had training or extensive practical experience in a discipline such as architecture, product design, graphic design, or interaction design' (Zimmermann et al. 2007, 493). And I will use the term 'designerly ways' (Cross 2001) to refer to mindsets, strategies and processes that, albeit not necessarily individually exclusive to, are together characteristic of, design methodologies—that is, how designers work and why. When experts in other fields of practice, such as sociolegal researchers, take up these designerly ways I will refer to them as approaching their work 'in design mode' (Manzini 2015).

Many before me have explored how design can enhance expert practices in other fields across the private, public and civil society sectors. Industry leaders such as the Design Council, IDEO and Stanford's d.school have for several decades promoted the export of designerly ways, often under the banner of 'design thinking', for use in a wide range of commercial and policy contexts (see, for example, Dorst et al. 2016; Kimbell 2011), while the subfield of Legal Design[1] emerged out of efforts to apply

DOI: 10.4324/9780367177683-1

information design techniques to make individual contracts more accessible (Brunschwig 2001; Haapio and Passera 2013) and then to apply service design techniques to make legal systems more 'usable, useful and engaging' (Hagan 2017). Today, designerly mindsets, strategies and processes are applied across the legal spheres of practice, activism and policy making (Perry-Kessaris 2019). And some have investigated how designerly ways might contribute to scholarly research beyond design (see Julier and Kimbell 2016). But there exists no sustained introduction to what it might mean to do non-design research in design mode, and what might be the risks and rewards. This volume addresses these questions through the example of sociolegal research. In so doing, it lays the foundations for the same to be done in relation to other disciplines.

Many before me have explored sociolegal research methods—that is, how we (ought to) use conceptual and empirical strategies to approach our substantive field of inquiry (see Banakar and Travers 2005; Creutzfeldt et al. 2019). But these treatments tend to be in the form of case studies and edited collections rather than sustained accounts. Importantly, there exists no generally agreed methodological narrative that integrates consideration of how individual research strategies (ought to) fit into wider processes, and how these (ought to) fit with deeper, norm-infused mindsets that (ought to) motivate and sustain our sociolegal research. It is also noteworthy that, despite concerns around training having circulated within the sociolegal community for well over a decade (Genn et al. 2006; Adler 2007), there are few sustained conversations about how we (ought to) teach research methods or why. We are not alone here: A recent study found deep pedagogical thoughtfulness, but limited systematic knowledge, among those delivering training across the social sciences in the UK and beyond (Nind and Lewthwaite 2019).

If we want to know what design can do for sociolegal research these questions are unavoidable. So, in exploring the proposition that we can and ought to do sociolegal research in design mode, this volume necessarily goes beyond introducing shiny new methods. It also confronts deeper questions around what sociolegal research is or ought to be and how we (ought to) do it, as well as why and for whom.

This chapter begins with an account of the intensive and curiosity-driven process of learning-by-doing through which I, a sociolegal researcher, came to hunt for methodological intersections between design and sociolegal research. It then identifies three challenges that face all sociolegal researchers—working with indeterminacy, generating meaningful change and engaging in meaningful relations, and three designerly ways that might enhance our ability to meet them—mindsets that are simultaneously practical-critical-imaginative, experimental processes and strategies that make things visible and tangible. The chapter ends with the proposition that together these designerly ways can contribute to the generation of enabling ecosystems that can enhance our ability to understand and meet sociolegal research challenges.

From visual communication to research through design

It requires 'little courage or originality ... to point out that a problem or issue can be addressed only in an interdisciplinary manner'. The challenge is to realize the aspiration, especially in 'institutional settings' (Klein 1996, 209). My own interest in design arose out of a frustration with what I perceived as ineffective communication among researchers working on questions of law and development—that is, how law shapes and is shaped by economic life, especially in relatively poor countries. For example, I argued that although 'approaches to law and development need not be uniform', they must at least 'take note of, place themselves in relation to, and build upon, each other', so we ought to try harder to 'pool the concepts, facts, and values that are characteristic of law, economics, and sociology to produce a con-nected, econo-sociolegal, approach' (Perry-Kessaris 2014a, 197). For those who specialize in epistemology and the history of knowledge, this is not a novel observation. For they know contemporary academia to be 'a house in which the inhabitants are leaning out of ... many open windows'—some 'happily chatting', others 'arguing' and still 'others have fallen out the win-dows' altogether; while inside the building, '[m]any doors remain closed' and others 'have been broken down', and just down the street, 'entirely new buildings have been constructed' (Klein 1996, 19). But it ought to be a source of continuous concern to soicolegal researchers as they go about their fundamentally interdisciplinary work.

It seemed to me that visual methods might help to transcend disciplinary boundaries by making concepts, facts and values more, or at least differ-ently, accessible, and by placing multiple perspectives in shared spaces. I decided to explore what graphic design, which is about visual communi-cation, can do for law. I chose to do so as a participant-observer not only because I wanted to acquire expert visual communication skills, but also because I wanted to access the dramatic shifts of perspective that can (only?) be gained by immersion in a new disciplinary ecosystem that I had previously experienced as a part-time student of economics. So I completed a few short courses, assembled a basic portfolio of designs and gained entry to a part-time postgraduate certificate in Design for Visual Communication at London College of Communication.

Over the course of an exhilarating and humbling year, I learned through looking—at typefaces, buildings, people, signage and posters—and through

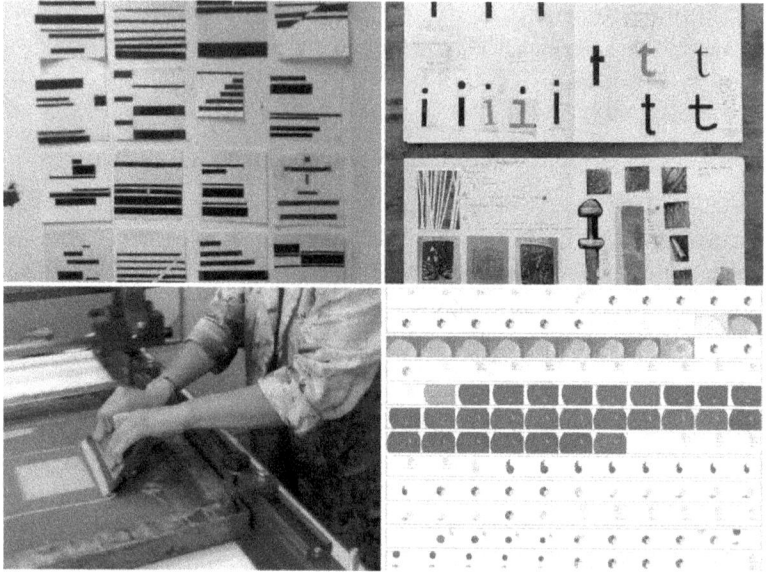

Figure 1.1 Scenes from a Postgraduate Certificate in Visual Communication, London College of Communication, 2014. Clockwise from top left: Displaying visual grammar tests, sketchbook entries documenting visual research into typographic and organic and inorganic shapes, screen printing and detail of a storyboard for a video on colour theory. Images: Amanda Perry-Kessaris.

making, with printing presses, binding twine, paper, scissors, pencils, clay, ink, glue, sticky notes, bodies, digital editing software and programming code, as well as through showing works in progress (Figure 1.1). As I completed weekly hands-on tasks, I learned how the principles of visual grammar, colour theory and semiotics impact the communication of legal messages; that an indirect benefit of designing visual communications is that we are forced to pay unusually close attention to exactly what we want to communicate, and to whom; and that visual communication can be as exclusionary and disabling as any other medium when designers fail to anticipate and accommodate a potential user's perceptions, expectations and experiences. An example of the impact of these insights on my socio-legal practice was *What can graphic design reveal about law?* An online interactive exhibit of my own designs, each expressing a perception or expectation of law, using just the word itself, and intended to provoke and facilitate conversation within academia and beyond about law, design and law and design.[2] But the deepest insight afforded to me by these experiences was that designers do things differently. I noticed an explicit emphasis on experimentation, which was entirely new to me; and that the emphasis on communication which initially drew me to graphic design also leads to an enrichment in interpersonal relations, especially through processes of continuous communal critique of visible and tangible work in progress .

These first forays into design left me as much chastened as emboldened and, therefore, ready for more. I went on to complete a part-time master's degree in Graphic Media Design—a programme with a curriculum aimed at exploring 'the use of graphic design as a critical tool to investigate the complexities of contemporary society'. In the terminology of Christopher Frayling (1993), my training in design for visual communication had left me with an appreciation for the idea of research *for* design—for example, exploring typefaces or paper stock to support the development of a new visual communication about law—and research *into* design, for example, exploring archives to understand how designs/ers work. This second round of training would focus my attention on how we can research *through* design. Over the ensuing two years, I responded to briefs inviting me to, for example, work collaboratively to 'edit/write, design and publish a short story' for a street market in east London, 'to be presented on-site'; 'formulate a critique and articulate a position' through a designed visual essay; design a digital commentary grounded in close engagement with an archival artefact; collaboratively interview a designer, and document it in a designed video; in relation to each brief, design a critical, visualized reflection on my process; and individually and collaboratively design exhibitions of works in progress and final outputs (Figure 1.2).[3] These were, once again, exciting and unnerving times. I was 'frustrated', for example, 'by my shallow visual library' and 'inadequate' technical skills, as well as by the challenge of producing designs that were 'both visually and intellectually clear, … widely useable but also meaningful'. More significantly, it took me some time to understand how my research programme had shifted. Now I was doing sociolegal research in design mode (Personal Fieldnotes).

Over time I began to widen my exploration of the potential risks and rewards of doing sociolegal research in design mode through a series of three types of activities—some individual, others participatory or collaborative—involving a total of over 200 predominantly sociolegal researchers. Each activity was grounded in the three designerly 'emphases' that I had identified during my studies in graphic design: Experimenting, communicating and relating. First, I mirrored my ongoing experience as a student of design by incrementally re-orienting the postgraduate Research Methods in Law module at Kent Law School around tasks, akin to design briefs, each of which invited students to experiment with different aspects

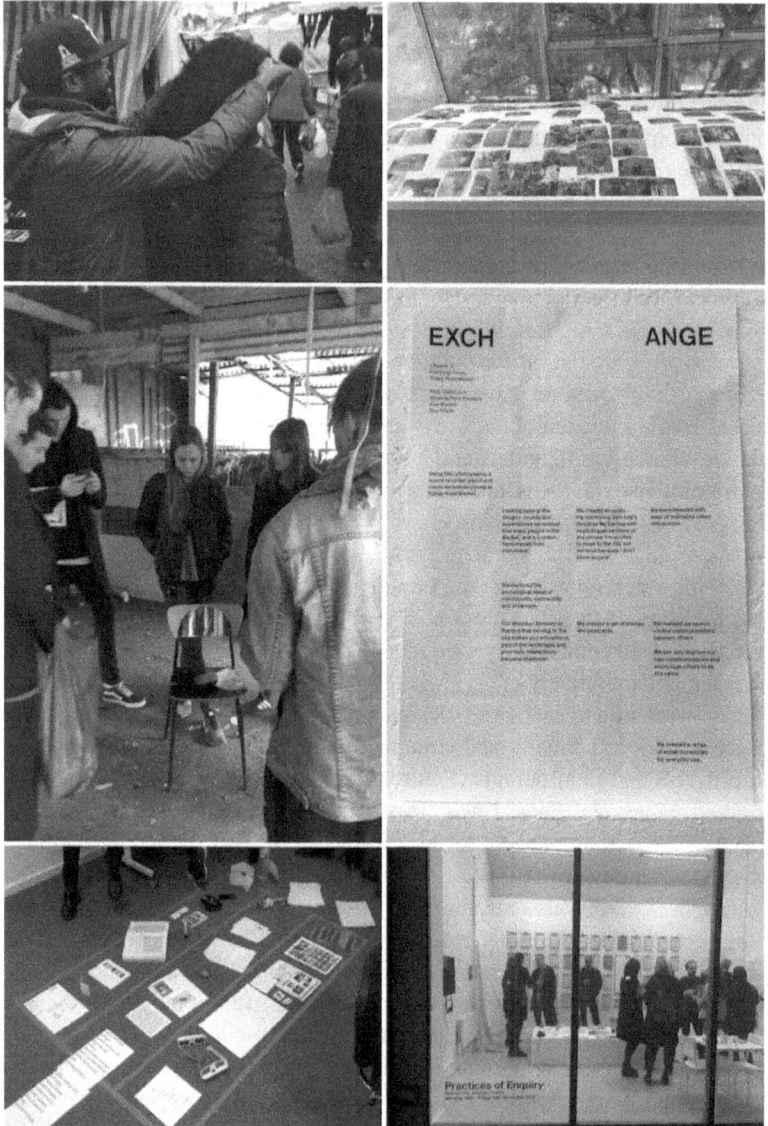

Figure 1.2 Scenes from an MA in Graphic Media Design, London College of Communication, 2015–2017. Clockwise from top left: Collecting and analyzing primary data for EXCHANGE, a short story published on-site, in text and audio format, in and for Ridley Road street market (see Perry-Kessaris 2016a); then co-designing and attending an exhibition of the making of that story. Images: Amanda Perry-Kessaris.

of their own research project. They exhibited the results on seminar room walls, or in models formed of building blocks, and we explored them together in the manner of a design 'crit'. Second, I (co-)designed a series of hands-on events in which groups of up to 50 other researchers explored their ideas through various modes of model making and observed them understanding and sharing their projects in new and productive ways. Third, I increasingly conducted my own research, which addresses the economic life of law, in design mode. For example, I used LEGO and clay to plan the central argument of an article and develop an appropriate language for approaching a sensitive field of inquiry (see Perry-Kessaris 2017a, b). Some of these activities, including participant feedback, are explored in Chapters 3 and 5 of this volume. All of them contributed to the evidence base underpinning the final component of my MA in Graphic Media Design—the *Sociolegal model-making* project—which centred on a downloadable guide indented to provoke and facilitate any sociolegal researcher anywhere to engage in the designerly strategy of making three-dimensional models (Sociolegal Model Making website). More broadly, this experimentation confirmed that it is possible to do, and to prompt and facilitate others to do, sociolegal research in design mode. Participants generally reported that working in design mode had positive impacts on their research and research relations, and these rewards seemed to out-weigh the risks of, for example, alienating sociolegal researchers or dis-tracting them from their core concerns.

The following sections place these empirical findings in the context of literature from sociolegal studies and design. They centre on two ques-tions: What challenges do we face as sociolegal researchers and how might designerly ways enhance our ability to understand and address them?

Sociolegal ways

The first step towards understanding how designerly ways might help us to understand and address sociolegal challenges is to identify the meth-odological underpinnings of sociolegal research (Figure 1.3). These can be explored along three interrelated dimensions. What, substantively, is researched; how—conceptually, empirically, analytically and processu-ally—it is researched; and, normatively, why—for what purposes and peo-ples—it is researched (Perry-Kessaris 2013).

What?

The substantive focus or 'what' of individual sociolegal studies varies widely because any research activity that is concerned with the 'mutually

WHY
values
interests

WHAT
text
context
subtext

HOW
conceptual
framework

HOW
empirical
data + tools

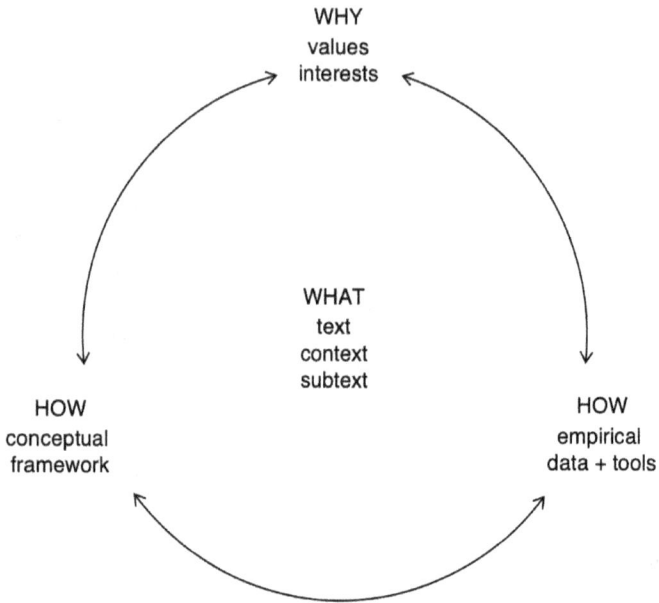

Figure 1.3 The questions that (ought to) lie at the heart of sociolegal research.
Image: Amanda Perry-Kessaris.

constitutive relationships between law and society' can be categorized as
sociolegal (Creutzfeldt et al. 2019, 3). Such studies address different legal
fields—for example, informal, local, national, regional, transnational and
international, and/or the relationships between them. They focus on different levels of social life—for example, micro-level actions of, and meso-
level interactions between individual actors, macro-level systems formed
by sustained interactions, meta-level rationalities that are shared by individuals and/or on mutually constitutive relationships between those different
levels of social life. They focus on law's roles in different social fields—for
example, on instrumental relations such as commercial trade and public
investment, on relations grounded in shared beliefs, on emotional relations,
on traditional or customary relations and/or on the interactions between
those different fields of social life. As the following section explains in
more detail, of particular relevance to this exploration of what design can do
for sociolegal research is that a substantial body of sociolegal scholarship
now focuses on surfacing relationships between legal, visual and material
worlds.

How?

To take a sociolegal approach is to commit to making, and communicating, a sense of law as a social phenomenon. This commitment imposes widely acknowledged conceptual constraints, in the sense that we can no longer think, for example, of law on the one hand and society on the other. It also imposes widely accepted empirical constraints, in the sense that, for example, we must look out not only for law on the books but also for the life of law—law in action. And law can, as a matter of plain fact, only meaningfully be understood as a social phenomenon if we attend to its real-world dimensions. 'You could never guess from the discourse of the jurists what their high-flown words really meant in context, or what practical meaning and effect legal doctrine would have once married to the realities of the established order in society' (Unger 2021, 3). So those who cleave to the theoretical, the abstract and the technical ought to consider their position. In the bracing words of economist Deidre McCloskey:

> An inquiry into the world must think and it must look. It must theorize and must observe. Formalize and record ... Not everyone ... needs do both ... But the inquiry as a whole must reflect and must listen. Both. Of course.
>
> (2002, 37)

Within these parameters, an ever-expanding variety of methods familiar to the social sciences and humanities is generally accepted as 'sociolegal'. A sociolegal study may be more or less conceptual versus empirical. Conceptual components maybe more or less radical or critical; and borrow from a wide range of conceptual framings including queer, historiographic, spatial, economic and so on. Empirical components may take the form of intimate case studies and oral histories or wide-ranging narratives; and draw on interviews, surveys, focus groups, site visits and archival work. And studies as a whole may be more or less quantitative and/or qualitative. An important implication of this growing menu of options is that we must take ever-more explicit responsibility for the methodological decisions that we make in all phases of our research—conceptualisation, data gathering, analysis, communication, reflection.

Of particular relevance in the present context is that some sociolegal researchers are purposefully using visual and material methods.[4] I will highlight three such uses. First, and most obviously, sociolegal researchers are using visual and material methods to communicate about their research—including illustrations, diagrams and photographs in presentations and formal research outputs—and visualizing entire research projects in posters. For example, SLSA annual conferences have attracted ever-more sophisticated contributions to the poster sessions introduced in 2012 (Figure 1.4), and some have turned the requirement to pre-record presentations for the virtual conferences of the current pandemic era into an opportunity to experiment with the moving image, including to reflect on their research process (Figure 1.5; see also Williams undated). And a thriving community of scholarship exists around expressing legal ideas in comic format (see Giddens 2015).

Second, as it becomes ever-more widely accepted that there can 'be no world and no subject … no public, no imagined community' and '[n]o state or nation or law or sovereign without the representations that bring them into existence' (Manderson 2019, 16), so sociolegal researchers are using methods from the humanities to analyse legal visuality and materiality, meaning 'what law looks'—and feels—'like' (Mulcahy 2017, S113. See also Resnick and Curtis 2011).[5] Some focus on the mutually constitutive relationships between the visual, the material and social lives of law. For example, Linda Mulcahy has used architectural analysis to reveal how court design influences relationships among those who 'use' the courts and the wider public sphere (Mulcahy 2011; Mulcahy and Rowden 2019); Marie-Andre Jacob and Anna Macdonald (2019) have combined sociolegal analysis and embodied dance practices to understand the combined affective and regulatory effects of a typographic device: the strikethrough; and The Art/Law Network seeks to offer a 'space where lawyers, activists, academics, thinkers of all creeds, can learn new open forms of law and legal thinking through bringing art into law' (The Art/Law Network website).[6] Others are joining sociologists of the environment, material culture and animals to decentre human accounts, and to give 'a central role to things/ objects/materials' both epistemologically, by treating them as valid sources of knowledge in their own right, and ontologically, by treating them as integral to and entangled with social life (Woodward 2020, 29. See further in Kang and Kendall 2019; Hohman and Joyce 2017; Perry-Kessaris 2017a).

Third, some are using visual and material methods to understand the social life of law more generally. For example, they use images and objects in interviews and in more participatory settings to 'draw out' and/ or to 'anchor' emergent 'narratives, comments or experiences', or to act as 'spaces of encounter' and 'points of connection' in the sense that knowledge is co-produced by interviewers and interviewees as they collaboratively interact with the images and objects, knowledge is co-produced (Woodward 2020, 34–7, 39–40, 42–3 and 85). For example, Leslie Moran (2015) has used judicial images not only as a source of data about judges and judicial institutions but also as a tool for eliciting responses from interviewees. Such

Figure 1.4 Poster submitted to SLSA Annual Conference 2020 that emerged out of a collaboration between a postgraduate researcher and a former child soldier turned activist, and which aims to bring the voices of child soldiers, including girls, into the international discourse. Sandhar and Omony (2019) '"I am free from the conflict, but I do not feel free": Experiences of child soldiers in Northern Uganda'. Illustrator Jennifer N R Smith.

Figure 1.5 Stills from a video diary through which two postgraduate researchers, by Danish Sheikh and André Dao, sought to 'capture fragments of a reading project that emerged from a disenchantment with critical theory' (Personal correspondence) in their presentation 'Translating dark into bright: Diary of a post-critical year' at the SLSA Annual Conference 2021, hosted online by Cardiff Law School.

strategies have the potential to surface 'far more' than an 'entirely verbal approach' (Mannay 2016, 41). Most recently, some sociolegal researchers are tapping into 'the playful capacity of things' to invite people to partici-pate—to 'interact, respond and join in', and their 'exciting' and productive capacity to introduce unpredictability into a research process (Woodward 2020, 54 and 72).[7] One example is the *Law in Children's Lives* project led by Dawn Watkins. Here a digital game was developed with the close and iterative participation of children and experts in childhood as a 'first step towards' developing resources to 'increase [children's] legal knowledge' and 'develop their legal capabilities'. Information provided by children during focus groups was used to generate 'everyday "worlds"' such as 'a school, a park, a shop and a friend's house' within the game, each of which was the site for 'law-related hypothetical scenarios or vignettes' (Watkins et al. 2018, 77–8. See also Mcdermont 2018; McKeever and Royal-Dawson 2021; Perry-Kessaris and Perry 2020). In deploying these visual and material ways, sociolegal researchers are already moving towards doing sociolegal research in design mode.

How do sociolegal researchers bring together and synthesize the conceptual and empirical insights that they generate through these various methods? Sociolegal researchers tend to rely on deductive and, to a lesser extent, inductive modes of analysis. To think deductively is to begin with theories—what we already 'know'. We draw on those theories to hypothesize about how things might be in different situations, and then confirm or reject that hypothesis through further investigation. When we think inductively, we seek from the outset to continuously 'ground' our theories in particular observations (Bryman 2016, 21 and 572–81). Both deductive and inductive methods are crucial to the incremental development of knowledge because they 'establish relations between already known constructs' (Kovács and Spens 2005, 135–7). Much of this volume is the product of these modes of analysis—the deductive work of drawing on design literature to theorize about what working in design mode might mean for sociolegal researchers and some more inductive ethnographic and auto-ethnographic exploratory activities.

Deductive analysis is well suited to explanation and justification— 'taking apart'. It is less well suited to 'making something new' (Cottam 2018, 221). An excessive reliance on deduction can lead to us behaving like 'lone warriors', 'heroically' seeking 'total control over' our field of interest, beginning sentences with 'of course'. At a group level, we begin to 'shape our identity around' the 'established practices' of our communities and become impervious to external influence (Dorst 2015, 13–8). When we treat these practices as 'sacred', it becomes difficult to make anything other than the utilitarian 'use' of them. We can implement them as they are, but we cannot 'play' with them. And play we must if we are to keep open the possibility of change (Agamben and Fort 2007). Science and technology studies tell us that research methodologies 'not only describe but also help to produce the reality they understand'. When we 'work on the assumption that the world is properly to be understood as', and therefore through, 'a set of fairly specific, determinate, and more or less identifiable processes', we risk elevating that which already dominates and stifling the actual/potential rest (Law 2004, 4–5). Stuckness sticks. An important result of 'stuckness' is we tend to narrow down too soon. For example, we define our 'problem' prematurely, and we do not stop to ask, 'what if', all of which can 'lead to suboptimal or even counterproductive solutions' (Dorst 2015, 12).

Although we sociolegal researchers are working to produce something new promising and hoping to engage in transformative or 'ground-break-ing' research, we are also wary of the uncertainty associated with such indeterminate ventures, tending to frame it as both 'avoidable and to be avoided' (Akama et al. 2018, 22). And, whether due to space constraints, doubts as to relevance, or fears of undermining the project's credibility, we prefer to present the selection and implementation of our research meth-ods as pre-defined and linear, rarely reporting the 'false starts, blind alleys, mistakes and enforced changes' that shape our projects (Bryman 2016, 13. See also Townsend and Burgess 2009).[8] Sociolegal researchers interviewed by Kritzer (2009) advised that indeterminacy and uncertainty it engenders becomes manageable when we commit to making a plan and amending it as necessary. However, it is rare to find formal and specific discussion of exactly how to go about being provisional or multiple—how, for example, simultaneously to make the plan and commit to amending it.

Sociolegal research is and ought to be laced with indeterminacy. This is, first, because that is the nature of all research, and second, as we shall see in more detail in the following because that is the nature of the wider world that we seek to understand and perhaps to influence. But this indeterminacy is not always explicitly recognized or well managed, let alone embraced or even activated.

Designerly ways can help.

Why?

Why—for what purposes—do we engage in sociolegal research?

We can surely agree that we aim to contribute something meaningful—in the dual sense of significant and valuable; and further that, in order to be meaningful, a contribution must have the potential to improve our ability to make and communicate a sense of law as a social phenomenon. But what does improvement look like? The UK Research Excellence Framework cri-teria for assessing research tell us to look not only for 'rigour' but also for 'originality' and 'significance' and separately seek to chivvy us towards contributions that generate wide-reaching and deep 'impact' in the wider world. But these are superficial and generic guides. For more specific direc-tion we can look to *Sociological Jurisprudence: Juristic Thought and Social Inquiry*, in which Cotterrell (2018) asserts that anyone who works with law, but especially sociolegal researchers, has a moral obligation to nurture and promote the 'well-being of law as a practical idea', including its 'worth' and 'meaningfulness as a social institution'. At first glance, the emphasis on 'practical' suggests this is a restatement of the previously mentioned requirement for empiricism. However, the notion of 'well-being' implies a deeper purpose that ought to direct sociolegal research methods and it implies a need for coherence in the service of multiplicity. There is widespread, albeit not universal, agreement that the fundamental purpose of law is to offer certainty and justice to 'all those living within [its] jurisdiction', and 'communicat[ing]', sometimes 'forcefully', the 'need for adequate and equal respect for [their] autonomy and dignity' (Cotterrell 2018, 31, 38 and 170). Often expressed in terms of the Rule of Law, this purpose of supporting certainty and justice can be thought of as a global constant. But there is a twist: The criteria with which to determine law's wellness—its actual fitness for that purpose—are as varied as the people, (inter)actions, systems and rationalities that shape law and are shaped by it. 'The idea of society is indeterminate'—not fixed—'even when it is idealized. No particular ordering of social life is natural or necessary. None enjoys uncontested authority' (Unger 2021, 19). The sociolegal is and ought to be a 'pluriverse' (Escobar 2017). Furthermore, every person participates in and across multiple, varied, fluid, overlapping, social networks; and each of us has multiple perspectives, expectations and experiences relating to law and its well-being. So, while working for the well-being of law as a practical idea can afford a certain energy, direction and sense of purpose, it is a necessarily multiple, fluid and, therefore, indeterminate—and, therefore, challenging—enterprise.

Indeed, to make and communicate the sense of law as a social phenomenon, in ways that support the well-being of law as a practical idea—as 'adapted to the specific, varying conditions of [its] sociohistorical existence'—might be 'the most distinctive' and 'ultimately the most difficult, form of legal expertise' (Cotterrell 2018, 31). It requires that we 'hold' the idea of law 'together' across these varied and shifting conceptual frameworks and empirical realities (Cotterrell 2018, 31). We must take a 'holistic approach' and 'be open to seeing links between seemingly unrelated realms that may raise non-intuitive relationships and interconnections' (Darian-Smith 2013, 15). Empirically, we must be able to move nimbly and assuredly across the micro, meso, macro and meta; the state, non-state, para-state and supra-state; the formal and the informal; the individual and the communal; the instrumental, affective, faith-based and traditional; the human, animal and ecological; the material and immaterial; the fun and frightening, stable and fleeting; and between pasts, presents and futures. Conceptually, we must adopt 'a theoretical sensibility', so that we can build the necessary language to communicate coherently with ourselves and with others, and so contribute to shared spaces. But we ought not to necessarily generate or adhere to any particular grand theory. This is not only because they tend to collapse on contact with the multiple empirical realities, but also because, as the jurisprudence of difference has long reminded us, we researchers are not and need not all be 'engaged in the same inquiry, about the same legal experience, with the same ends in view' (Cotterrell 2018, 162). Rather, we must be 'eclectic and creative' (Darian-Smith 2013, 15. See also Escobar 2017, xvi), generating or borrowing vocabulary and grammar and 'bricolag[ing]' it into a 'general but flexible practical framework of thought—a way of envisaging or modelling law as a phenomenon, at least provisionally in relation to' a given 'time and place'. And we ought to treat any resulting 'model' or 'framework … less as making a "claim to truth" … than as' a way of 'organising efforts towards solving specific problems' (Cotterrell 2018, 33, 99 and 162). The aim is to achieve 'coherence' rather than uniformity—not to merge these multiplicities, but rather to 'gather' them together provisionally into shared spaces (Law 2004, 100).

If we are to manage, let alone activate, indeterminacy we must first acknowledge that all research is wandering and serendipitous, 'messy' and therefore itself indeterminate (Law 2004. See also Bryman 2016, 13). Then we must commit to embracing and activating that indeterminacy by being more 'multiple', more 'modest', more 'uncertain', more 'diverse' (Law 2004, 9). We must 'unmake' our bad 'methodological habits' such as our 'depend[ence] on the automatic', our 'desire for certainty', our 'belief that we have special insights that allow us to see further than others' and our expectation that we will 'arrive at more or less stable' and generalizable 'conclusions about' how 'things really are' (Law 2004, 11). In short, we need to be less determined, more provisional.

Designerly ways can help.

For whom?

We can also surely agree that any academic research ought to be for, or aimed at, making some contribution within academia. If not there, where; if not that, what? Research proposals and outputs that do not specify how they might contribute, for example, to creating, highlighting and/or resolving misconceptions in existing scholarship are less likely to be funded, published, read or lauded by 'the' sociolegal community. And we may also aim to contribute to the wider world. Today, this idea is associated with the contemporary 'impact' agenda, which some see as part of an oppressive and damaging trend towards the marketization and auditing of public spaces. But all research—even that which seeks 'only' to describe, predict and explain—has the capacity to impact upon real-world perceptions, expectations and experiences. Edward Said argued that '[e]very intellectual whose métier is articulating and representing specific views, ideas, ideologies, logically aspires to making them work in a society' so any 'who claims to write only for him or herself, or for the sake of pure learning, or abstract science is not to be, and *must not* be, believed' (1994, 110). Bagele Chilisa goes further to argue that research must be designed 'to challenge existing power structures in order to transform lives' within and beyond research communities (2012, 22 and 174–5. See also Tuhiwai Smith 2012). But the perceptions, expectations and experiences of those within and beyond research communities are multiple and fluid. This amplifies the indeterminacy of the sociolegal research enterprise, including what might constitute a meaningful contribution or relationship, and how to make it happen.

As the SLSA's Statement of Principle of Ethical Research Practice of 2009 reminds us, we must attend not only to the importance of 'integrity and quality in conducting research'—including, for example, of crediting contributions made by colleagues and collaborators—but also to the wider 'value [of] collegiality in the sociolegal community'. A sense of community can emerge out of any form of relatively stable interactions centring on shared values and interests, but only if those interactions are grounded in feelings of belonging and mutual interpersonal trust (Cotterrell 2018, 163). Who is (not) able to engage in stable and trusting relations around sociolegal research, and so to feel, and be seen as, a member of 'the' sociolegal community? We know that the academic population in the UK does not reflect the wider population of the UK, let alone the wider world that it researches. Of all professors across all disciplines in the UK in 2019, 3.2 per cent were disclosed as disabled, 23.6 per cent were white women, 7.7 per cent were men of colour and 2.3 per cent were women of colour (Advance 2019a, b). The majority of higher education institutions in the UK employed not one female professor of black or minority ethnic origin in any discipline in 2017, and in law, there were just six women of colour employed as law professors in the UK (Solanke 2017). A great deal of intellect, time, energy and emotion has been put into explaining how and why we fail to 'include', why it matters, pragmatically and morally, and how we might do better (Ahmed 2012; Memon and Jivraj 2020). We know that to be genuinely communal, the spaces that we generate must be 'meaningful, relevant and accessible to all' actual and potential participants, and that this requires the anticipation and proactive 'valuing' of difference (Hockings 2010). Just as law must gather, nurture and protect all its peoples, so must legal research communities.

Whether or not we aim for our research to contribute to wider social life, we must take responsibility for the fact that it is part of it. We must, of course, do this by way of ethical approval processes that focus on the impact that any entanglement in our research—as subject matter informant, participant or collaborator—may have. But there is more to it than that: '[I]n the course of their activities', sociolegal researchers 'enter into personal and moral relationships with those whom they study closely'—whether 'individuals, households, social groups or corporate entities'. And '[w]henever possible, research relationships should be characterised by trust' (SLSA 2009).[9]

So the work of making meaningful contributions through sociolegal research is 'about more' than methods and methodology and more than how the social world is or ought to be. 'It is also, and most fundamentally, about a way of being' (Law 2004, 10). Here 'being' is about how we relate to ourselves and our projects, how we relate to others within and beyond our sociolegal research community and whether and how those two ways of being reflect and sustain each other. For example, when we are assessing the well-being of law we might ask whether it tends to function as a 'communal', as opposed to solely 'private' or 'individual', 'resource for channelling power'. Is law supporting mutual interpersonal trust within and between communities—by expressing whatever varied values and interests hold us together, by coordinating the varied values and interests that hold us apart and by provoking and facilitating participation by all in varied forms of communal life (Cotterrell 2006; Perry-Kessaris 2008)? Is it prompting, facilitating and sustaining unity from and for diversity? Likewise, in assessing the meaningfulness of sociolegal research, we ought to ask whether we are supporting trusting relations within and beyond the sociolegal community by expressing what holds us together, coordinating what holds us apart and encouraging participation.

Designerly ways can help.

Designerly ways

The next step towards understanding how designerly ways might help us to understand and address sociolegal challenges is to identify the methodological underpinnings of design—beginning with its substantive focus. Design is, perhaps above all things, about change:

> It seems like designers always want the world to be different. And even when it's not the specific desire of designers themselves to spark a particular change, designers and the practices of design are constantly being brought to bear by others to initiate change.
>
> (DiSalvo 2016, 29)

Change for what purpose? Why, and with and for whom? We can think of designers as aiming for change that is meaningful, in the dual sense of being both significant and valuable. I choose 'meaningful change' in part because

I want to maintain some distance from some of the 'dark sides' historically associated with the term 'innovation'—specifically, its emphasis on change for the sake of it; on aggregated costs and benefits over micro-disparities and diversities in perceptions, expectations and experiences; and on neoliberal values such as efficiency, maximization and growth (see further in Fougère and Eija Meriläinen 2021; Julier 2017). In our anthropocentric world, the value or meaningfulness of a change tends to be assessed according to human perceptions, expectations and experiences around a combination of beauty and functionality. But questions of what is beautiful, what functions and, therefore, what is meaningful are dependent upon, for example, the perspectives of designers and users, and the context within which a design is designed occurs. The following paragraphs trace some key moments in the evolution of these perspectives and contexts, and how these moments have influenced both designerly ways, and how those designerly ways are understood.

Design has long been closely, albeit not exclusively, associated with 'functionalist, rationalistic, and industrial' aims (Escobar 2017, x; Perry-Kessaris 2020). The pioneering Preliminary Course (*Vorkurs*) at the Bauhaus school of art and design—which built on the Arts and Crafts Movement and continues to influence how design is taught and practised globally to this day—aimed to systematize design methods and design pedagogy, in particular by using 'practical, concrete exercises' to emphasize the importance of 'process' (Saletnik 2007). These practices travelled to the Ulm School of Design (*Hochschule für Gestaltung* 1953–1968) where course leaders explicitly sought 'to make the design process more readily accessible and easy to understand'. And their objective here was not only to improve design as a discipline, but also 'to facilitate cross-disciplinary work, for example, with anthropology and psychology' (Oswald 2012, 68). Thereafter, this systematization agenda persisted in the design methods movement that came to dominate in the 1960s.

At the same time, some designers increasingly promoted design as a resource for other disciplines—not only to improve how those disciplines function internally, but also to improve how they interact with each other. Most famously, political scientist and cognitive psychologist Herbert A. Simon declared in 1969 that design is/ought to be a systematic, 'process-oriented activity' for solving a wide array of problems, and, moreover, that as a problem-solving 'science', design could act as a 'glue' to hold the social sciences together (Huppatz 2015, 29. See also Bayazit 2004; Charman 2010, 29). In 1973, Horst Rittell and Melvin Webber (1973) sought to identify which kinds of ostensibly non-design situations or issues are especially well suited to a designerly approach. They declared that some problems are 'wicked problems'—that is, they involve the sometimes conflicting and

shifting perceptions, expectations and experiences of multiple stakeholders. Such problems, they argued, can only be addressed through designerly,
rather than 'reductionist' scientific approaches. In this way, they identified
'an opportunity for design research to provide complementary knowledge'
to that offered by other disciplines, and 'through methods unique to design'
(Zimmerman et al. 2007, 496. Emphasis added. See also Buchanan 1992).

More recently, such wicked problems have been described as 'dynamic,
open, complex and networked' (Dorst 2015, 6–12), and it has been argued
that one reason designerly ways are so well suited to addressing wicked
problems is that they prompt and facilitate abductive thinking. The notion
of 'abductive' thinking was developed by philosopher Charles Sanders
Pierce between 1878 and 1913 'as a means of finding out what exists in
the world' (Askeland 2020, 67). It was part of his new philosophical tradition of pragmatism, which is characterized by its adherence to the proposition that in assessing the meaningfulness of an idea—both analytical and
normative—we must take account of its practical consequences. Abductive
thinking can be thought of as a form of 'systematized creativity' (Kovács
and Spens 2005, 135–137) in which 'imagination, association and intuition' are combined to produce 'flashes' of insight (Askeland 2020, 66) into
'puzzling phenomena' (Hammersley 2016, 748). Judgement and decision-
making are suspended, provisionality is embraced (Dorst 2015, 49), and
both the 'problem' and the 'solution' are allowed to emerge. In this way,
'unfiltered and associative elements' may 'spontaneously emerge as knowing'. Such 'emergent' knowing may be 'intimate', not be 'publicly verifi-
able', 'independent' or grounded in theory or empirical proof and it 'might
only matter in that moment' and the researcher(s) in question (Akama et
al. 2018, 116–7). But it is, nevertheless, a way of knowing, and it can open
the door to new insights. We all engage in abductive thinking[10] when, for
example, we suddenly realize 'This is the research question to which I am
really seeking an answer!'; or 'This quote from this interviewee begins to
make sense when I place it next to, or categorize it with, that quote from that
interview!' It may happen on a furious walk, in repeated rewritings, while
watching a football match or in the reading of a poem. The presence and
potential of abductive thinking and resulting insights are generally under-
appreciated among natural and social scientists,[11] but philosophers of science note that 'advances … are often achieved' abductively—that is, not by
'logical process' but 'through an intuitive leap that comes forth as a whole'
and is triggered by an 'unexpected observation' or 'anomaly' (Kovács and
Spens 2005, 135–137). And this imaginative and provisional way of thinking is central to design practice because it is essential to the indeterminate
task of making new things, systems and so on (see Chapter 2). It is also
well suited to addressing 'wicked' problems because they are 'mess[y]',

'ambiguous', interconnected, 'unpredictable' and, therefore, indeterminate (Burns et al. 2005, 8), and consequently, resistant to conventional deduction and induction.

The final moment to which I wish to draw attention is a 2007 intervention by Human-Computer Interaction designers John Zimmerman, Jodi Forlizzi and Shelley Evenson, who revealed, albeit not quite explicitly, that much of design's potential as a resource for transdisciplinary research lies in its materiality, even sociomateriality. They proposed that 'making' is 'a method of inquiry' capable of directly addressing the kinds of 'wicked problems' that mainstream design was by now happy to accept as its home turf. They argued that both design artefacts, and the processes by which they are made, can generate knowledge (Zimmerman et al. 2007, 497). In so doing, they clarified two things about design and design research. First, they clarified how a designer might, specifically in their capacity as makers, collaborate with researchers from other disciplines (Zimmerman 2007, 496)—by making new conceptual frames for problems, making material representations of possible solutions and making records of the research process. Second, it clarified that design is more than 'a cognitive resource'. It is a sociomaterial practice—that is, an assemblage of mindsets, tools and processes that emerge from 'dynamic configurations of minds, bodies, objects, discourses, knowledge, structures/processes and agency' (Kimbell 2012, 134–6).[12] Because design is a sociomaterial practice, we are both 'designed by our designing' and also 'through our interactions with the structural and material specificities of our environments', we are designed 'by that which we have designed'. Anne-Marie Willis summarizes these relationships between humans and design as a 'double movement': '[W]e design our world'—that is, 'we deliberate, plan and scheme in ways which prefigure our actions and makings'; and 'our world acts back on', and 'designs', 'us'. So we must understand design 'ontologically' both in the abstract, conceptual sense that we can use design to think about the world; and in the concrete, pragmatic and moral sense that we ought to use design to advance, mitigate or avoid particular outcomes (Willis 2006, 80).

Contemporary designers tend to understand their purpose, their search for meaningful change, as entailing a mixture of, on the one hand, problem finding and solving—that is, with identifying how things do and might work, as a matter of function and utility—and, on the other hand, 'sense-making'—that is, with identifying how things are and could be understood, as a matter of form and beauty (Manzini 2015). They draw on methods familiar to social science and humanities such as literature review, interview, ethnographic observation, focus groups and so on to understand the characteristics, values and interests of those for whom their designs are meant; and they draw on visual and material methods from across the creative arts to make those designs a reality. What I want to highlight as distinctive of design is how they use those methods—with what mindsets, in the context of what processes and strategies.

The following sections introduce three designerly ways: Practical-critical-imaginative mindsets, experimental processes and visible and tangible communication strategies. Others will select different ways and use different terminology to capture them. My choices here are influenced not only by my research into design but also by my position as a sociolegal researcher seeking to influence the thinking and behaviour of others in my field. I focus on these ways in part because I have found them to be at once ostensibly alien and deeply relevant to sociolegal researchers.

Practical-critical-imaginative mindsets

Designers have variously been described in terms such as 'open' and sharing', devoted to 'continuous improvement' and 'tinkering' and likely to ask, 'not whether but how' (Cottam 2018, 239), or as 'empathetic', 'optimistic', full of 'creative confidence' and capable of 'embracing ambiguity' and 'learning from failure' (IDEO 2009, 10). Social innovation designer Ezio Manzini (2015) perhaps captured it best—most comprehensively, precisely and accessibly—when he proposed that designers are practical, critical and creative. Designers are, Manzini argues, critical in the sense that they can identify opportunities for change; they are creative, in the sense that they can envisage what the shape of those changes, and their effects, might be; and they are practical, in the sense that they can ensure that change is valuable to those who are implicated in and by it and that they can make it happen. Drawing on Amartya Sen and Martha Nussbaum's 'capability approach', Manzini proposes that all humans are inherently practical, critical and creative, and/but that these capabilities can be activated and enhanced if we operate in 'design mode' (2015).

Over time, I have come to substitute 'imaginative' for 'creative' because imagination seems to point more evenly towards thinking as well as making and, perhaps for this reason, it is, as we shall see, more commonly and easily referred to than creativity in the legal sphere. Furthermore, as I will explain in more detail in Chapter 2, I have argued that a designerly mindset is necessarily *simultaneously* practical-critical-imaginative and that the combined effect of these three dimensions of a designerly mindset is to afford a sense of openness and direction—of 'structured freedom' (Perry-Kessaris 2017a). To contextualize these propositions in wider, including legal, theories of knowledge, we can say that in a design context, the relatively practical and critical modes of deductive and inductive thinking are supplemented with a relatively imaginative mode of abductive thinking.

But to work in design mode requires more than a mindset. This practical-critical-imaginative orientation must be reflected in and sustained by processes and strategies.

Experimental processes, visible and tangible communication strategies

When we work in design mode, practical-critical-imaginative mindsets, and the sense of structured freedom that they generate, are reflected in, and sustained by, designerly processes that promote experimentation and strategies that emphasize visible and tangible communication.

Design is about making something new. The making of any new thing— an artefact, an argument—is a necessarily indeterminate enterprise. Ideas emerge from a 'process of growth'. Over time, various 'pieces ... gradually acquire a feel for each other', they '*settle*, holding each other in place ever more tightly', and so 'the work advances ... towards' a 'closure' of sorts (Ingold 2013, 21 and 69. Emphasis original). In the process, we 'organically and evolutionarily learn, discover, generate, and refine' (Lim et al. 2008, 2) our understanding of what, if anything, needs to be changed, what shape that change might take and how to make it happen; and each such understanding is susceptible to rejection or amendment in future iterations (see Malpass 2017, 88; Buchanan 1992, 16; Dorst 2015, 490). Indeterminacy, and the feelings of uncertainty that it provokes, can be distracting and debilitating, even distressing. But it is not all or always bad. Indeed, for designers, indeterminacy and associated feelings of uncertainty are a necessary, even 'familiar or comfortable way of being'. They are 'at the very centre of design practice, animating and propelling creative exploration'. Indeed, design anthropologists Yoko Akama, Sara Pink and Shanti Sumartojo argue that indeterminacy, and the feelings of uncertainty that it engenders, can afford three opportunities to designers. First, it may afford opportunities for 'disruption'—to defamiliarize oneself from, and to look afresh at, well-used concepts or well-known objects, places, people or relationships. Second, it may afford opportunities to 'surrender'—whether to contingency, to collaboration, to process or to chance. Third, it may afford opportunities to 'mov[e] beyond'—to step forwards to futures, backwards to pasts, sideways or behind to alternatives and so on (Akama et al. 2018, 22, 35–6 and 45–52).

What distinguishes designers from others, including sociolegal researchers, who seek to make new things is, first, that they access these affordances by meeting indeterminacy with explicit, proactive provisionality. And they keep that provisionality productive—maintain direction and avoid being overwhelmed by uncertainty—by structuring it within processes that promote experimentation. Here I am using experimentation both in 'the natural scientific sense of testing a preconceived hypothesis, or of engineering a confrontation between ideas "in the head" and facts "on the ground"', and 'in the sense of prising an opening and following where it leads' (Ingold 2013, 6–7). One example of such an experimental design process is an innovation design technique known as 'frame innovation'. This involves repeatedly 'zoom[ing] in and out' between a problem and its context to generate alternative possible 'frames' for a problem situation. The new frames, to be formulated in the pattern 'If ... as if ... then', then act as working propositions from which to 'bridge' to a new approach (Dorst 2015; Dorst et al. 2016). Like practical-critical-imaginative mindsets, these processes introduce a sense of structured freedom: The freedom of provisionality structured by a strong impetus to do something, decide something, deliver something. In these ways, designers direct indeterminacy towards meaningful change.

The second distinguishing feature of designerly ways with indeterminacy is that they make things visible and tangible. In part as a consequence of the fact that the things they make—objects, images, spaces and so on—have a tendency to be visible and/or tangible, designers tend to adopt a strategy of communicating their ideas, to themselves and to others, in artefacts as they go along, as part of their experimental process. In short, designers use experimental making as a 'method of' individual and/or collaborative 'inquiry' (Zimmerman et al. 2007, 497):

> Through an active process of ideating, iterating, and critiquing potential solutions, design researchers continually reframe the problem as they attempt to make the *right* thing. The final output of this activity is a concrete problem framing and articulation of the preferred state, and a series of artifacts—models, prototypes, products, and documentation of the design process.
>
> (Zimmerman et al. 2007, 497)

By making things visible and tangible in this way, designers prompt and facilitate themselves to see and to think, and also to relate—that is, to collaborate and to build community—in ways that are less accessible through other disciplines.

Designerly processes and strategies tend to be intentionally 'lightweight and easy to grasp', and to 'filter complexity' through a narrow 'lens' of, for example, a specific 'user' or 'problem' (Stickdorn et al. 2018, 14). And/but note that it often takes a great deal of insight and skill to make simple, clear and accessible things, and there is no reason to assume that such things cannot generate profound insights. When combined with practical-critical-imaginative mindsets, these experimental processes and visible and tangible communication strategies contribute to generating potential 'enabling ecosystems' (Manzini 2015) within which we can be prompted and facilitated to access opportunities for disruption, surrender and moving beyond, and individually and collaboratively to make and communicate a sense of things in new and meaningful ways.

The sociolegal relevance of designerly ways

Looking through a designerly lens, we can better understand that to make meaningful contributions, and to engage in meaningful research relations, sociolegal researchers must be simultaneously practical, critical and imaginative. To make meaningful contributions towards the well-being of law as a practical idea, we must *be* practical—that is, we must identify 'feasible ways of getting things to happen.' And to do this we must be engaged in meaningful relations with real people, in real places, within academia and in the wider world. We must also be critical—that is, 'look at the state of things and recognise what cannot or should not be acceptable' (Manzini 2015, 31). It is through critique—'asking questions, making distinctions, restoring to memory all those things that tend to be overlooked or walked past in the rush to collective judgement and action' (Said 1994, 32–3)—that we become able to identify what might be in need of improvement and how. But we cannot be content to simply 'unmask or debunk' law (Cotterrell 2018, 32 and 33). If we were only to tear law down, lean back and survey the wreckage, offer no alternative vision, then we would not be working for law's well-being. We must remain open, even in the worst of times, to law's 'utopian, aspirational face' (Cotterrell 2002, 643). To do this, we must be imaginative—to conjure that which does not exist in our here and now (Manzini 2015, 31); to move beyond and between what has been, what is and what might yet be. Lawyerly types have long celebrated the many roles played by imagination in legal thinking and practice.[13] Some value imagination as a 'synthe[tic]' device, to generate coherent conceptualizations of what law—including the life of law—is. Some value imagination as an 'empath[etic]' device—a way of enhancing our ability to identify with others so that law can more effectively be deployed as an 'instrument of world-improvement'. Some value imagination as a 'transformative' or 'inventi[ve]' device—a way of generating new possibilities for and through law, as part of wider 'social imaginaries' and/or 'social realities'.[14] Finally, those who 'believe that a proper recollection of and care for the past makes a future possible', tend to value imagination as an 'attun[ing] device' (Antaki 2012, 8–14). Seen in this latter, 'nostalgic', light, the human capacity for imagination is not merely useful. It is a way of 'overcoming' what Max

Weber described as 'the fate of our times'—namely, to live lives that are 'characterized by rationalisation and intellectualization and above all, ... disenchantment' (Quoted in Antaki 2012, 2 and 4). It enhances our 'capacity to accept the gift of enchantment'—that is, the ability 'to be struck, to be arrested, to experience wonder' (Antaki 2012, 15). Designerly ways can enhance our ability to be, and to value being, imaginative in all of these respects.

Looking through a designerly lens, we can understand that sociolegal research tends to focus on wicked empirical and conceptual problems. They are dynamic, open, complex and networked—and, therefore 'mess[y]', 'ambiguous', interconnected and 'unpredictable' (Burns et al. 2005, 8), and, therefore, indeterminate. We can also understand that the processes through which we research those wicked problems are themselves necessarily indeterminate—they are a form of making, and the making continues when we communicate about our ideas with others and 'an eternal process of adaptation, maintenance and renewal begins' (Ingold 2013, 48). And that process is necessarily social, in the sense that research entails social interactions—it has a role to play in working for certain forms of social relations and it affects and is affected by wider social life (Perry-Kessaris 2020). And so, a designerly lens can also prompt and facilitate us to consider those whom we anticipated might 'use' our research, within and beyond the academic world, and how our contributions to, and relations with, them might be made more meaningful (see Norman [1988] 2013).

Proposition:
> If we were to approach sociolegal research as if it were a design problem then we could enhance our ability to make meaningful research contributions, and to engage in meaningful research relations, both within our research community and in the wider world.

What follows

This book is intended to change how sociolegal researchers think about their research and research relations. If it shifts how you think, then it will have made a meaningful contribution—all the more so if it also shifts your behaviour, irrespective of whether that shift goes with or against the grain of its core proposition. If you use it, you will adapt it—make it more meaningful, and therefore valuable to yourself and/or to others. Even if it is widely used, it will eventually be let go as new contributions take its place. This is the proper fate of almost all academic work.

Although the primary focus of this book is on what we might take from design back to the sociolegal research community, it also offers lessons to designers, especially those who work with law. First, it highlights points of contact between design and law—sites on which legal designers can productively focus to develop their thinking and practice to the benefit of both disciplines. Second, it offers persuasive grounds for arguing that legal designers should operate in the sociolegal mode (Perry-Kessaris 2020)—that is, with an analytical-empirical-normative commitment to understanding the legal and the social as mutually constitutive, and to promoting the well-being of law as a practical idea. They ought to think of themselves as sociolegal designers.

Chapter 2 sets out in more detail how designerly processes and strategies combine to generate practical-critical-imaginative, structured-yet-free, potentially enabling ecosystems. Those in search of specific examples of sociolegal researchers working in design mode will find them in Chapter 3, while examples of expert designers working on issues of sociolegal concern are explored in Chapter 4. Because this volume is intended to prompt and facilitate sociolegal researchers to do things differently, it closes with an opening—Chapter 5, 'Entering design mode'—where the impatient can make an immediate start on a series of accessible sociolegal design briefs.

Notes

1 A term coined by Colette Brunschwig in 2001 and popularized by Stefania Passera and Margaret Hagan in 2013.
2 The exhibition, #APKLawDesigns, is available under 'collections' at amandaperrykessaris.org.
3 Blog posts detailing each of these briefs are available at https://amandaperrykessaris.org.
4 Sophie Woodward (2020) coined the term 'material methods' and offered the first sustained, integrated account of the many ways in which materials and materiality can play a role in social science research.
5 The rise in digitalization and online life has brought highly visualizable immaterial sources such as big data and social media profiles (Creutzfeld et al. Part III) inside the sociolegal frame alongside tangible files and archives (Vismann 2008, Latour 2009).
6 An example of their practice was Union, a participatory exhibition in which 'sound, text, film and performance' were used to 'invite' members of the public 'to share their opinions and have their preconceptions challenged in advance' of the Brexit referendum (The Art/Law Network website).
7 On participatory research, see Bergold and Thomas (2012).
8 Indeed, most academic 'accounts' of research methods focus more on the individual strategies through which we 'collect' and 'manipulat[e]' data or materials and less on the overarching process (Law 2004, 4–5).
9 See also the Concordat for Research Integrity produced in 2012 (updated 2019) by Universities UK, UK Research and Innovation and Wellcome Trust and the Concordat for Engaging the Public with Research.

10 Researchers from across the social sciences and humanities investigate abductive thinking in the wider world, and some, ethnographers in particular, seek to emulate the abductive thinking of their research subjects as part of a wider effort to conduct research through their 'worldview' (Bryman 2016, 394).

11 Among doctrinal lawyers and legal practitioners, abductive thinking has generally been discussed in relation to evidentiary matters, which makes sense since this is their main point of contact with the empirical (Askeland 2020, 67). Sociologists Iddo Tavory and Stefan Timmermans (2014) have used the term abduction to describe 'an approach to qualitative data analysis that steers a course between data-driven inductivism, at one end of the spectrum, and a theory-driven or deductive mode of analysis, at the other'. Fellow sociologist Martin Hammersley draws attention to two weaknesses in their important contribution: they 'treat abduction as if it could stand alone' rather than 'complementary' to induction and deduction, and although presented as new, their approach is perhaps better seen as a purposeful gathering, foregrounding, buttressing and/ or activating of what many qualitative researchers already do (2016, 748).

12 This emphasis on the kinaesthetic generally and on embodied making in particular can be traced, at least in the Global North, to the late nineteenth-century Arts and Crafts Movement led by William Morris and the German Bauhaus school of art and design (1919–1933): Both emphasized the social, psychological and creative importance of bodies, and of making and engaging with artefacts (Weingarden 1985, Saletnik 2007, Perry-Kessaris 2020).

13 The 1973 publication of James Boyd White's *The Legal Imagination* was a 'pivotal moment' in the turn to imagination (Antaki 2012, 2).

14 The term 'social imaginaries' was coined by Cornelius Castoriadis (1975).

2 Enabling ecosystems

This chapter explores the proposition that designerly ways can generate enabling ecosystems. Enabling of what and whom? Design cannot answer the question for us. Designerly ways are often used—explicitly and implicitly, directly and indirectly—to promote dominant neoliberal values and interests to promote progressive change or radical transformation (see Johns 2019; Julier 2017), or as part of an introspective hacky or makerly personal life-style choice, rather than as part of an outward-looking, inclusive countercultural movement (See Davies 2018). Chapter 1 established that this book is specifically concerned with how designerly ways can enhance research into the well-being of law as a practical idea by any and all actual and potential members of the sociolegal research community. It then proposed that designerly ways can generate practical-critical-imaginative, structured-yet-free, potentially enabling ecosystems; and that within these ecosystems we might enhance our ability to understand and meet the sociolegal research challenges of working with indeterminacy, making meaningful research contributions and engaging in meaningful research relations. This chapter reveals more about how.

It begins with an analysis of perhaps the most common reference point for those approaching design from the outside, the Double Diamond, as an (imperfect) visualization of an enabling ecosystem. It then offers examples of enabling ecosystems drawn from two subfields, Social Design and Policy Design, to give a holistic and concrete sense of what is meant by 'enabling ecosystems'. It then explores in more depth each of the two aspects of enabling ecosystems that I am proposing are both central to designerly ways, and of particular interest to sociolegal researchers: First, how designers use experimental processes to progress provisionally, prompting and facilitating themselves to access the opportunities afforded by indeterminacy; then how, by making things visible and tangible, designers prompt and facilitate themselves to see, to think, to collaborate and to build community in new

DOI: 10.4324/9780367177683-2

ways. It ends with some caveats both about the limits of designerly ways and the technical capacity of sociolegal researchers to deploy them.

The Double Diamond

In 2004, in response to an explosion of external interest in the strategic potential of design as a transdisciplinary resource, the Design Council, which is an independent charity and advisor to the UK government on design, developed the Double Diamond (Figure 2.1). It was intended to demystify design by laying bare its 'universal' elements. Any claim to universality is bound to be falsifiable and exclusionary but, variance in textual and visual language aside, the myriad systems, toolkits and guides produced by globally leading design institutions certainly share a common core (Stickdorn et al. 2018, 21. See Toolbox Toolbox website). What the 2004 Double Diamond captures very well—iconically, in fact—is the idea that designerly ways can generate a potentially enabling ecosystem—'a container, a certainty in our foggy world' so that although 'we don't know the problem we will address or what we are going to create ... we do have a trusty vehicle for the journey' (Cottam 2018, 227). The Double Diamond does this primarily by surfacing the divergent and convergent rhythms that characterize design processes that help designers to progress: Discover, define, develop, deliver.

We can gain a sense of the explanatory power of the Double Diamond by narrating an idealized sociolegal research process through it. We begin with a concern, an issue, a topic, an example. We generate a field of inquiry. It is a time of discovery. We feel a sense of purpose, even exhilaration. Anything is possible and everything, including our point of departure, is open to

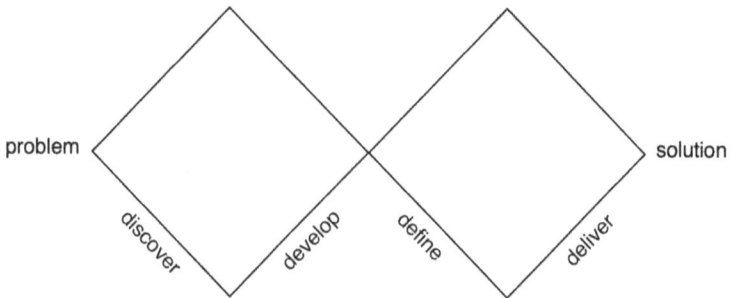

Figure 2.1 The 'universal' elements of design adapted by the author from the Double Diamond as originally developed by the Design Council in 2004 (Design Council website).

challenge. We have the courage to ask, 'what if'. As our field of inquiry grows, and our insights multiply, we begin to want to make sense of it all. Perhaps we worry that we have lost sight of where we began and where we thought we were going. We begin to search for a focal point towards which we can direct our initial insights. It is a time of definition. After multiple attempts, we settle on a more specific target—a question, a proposition, a hypothesis, a conjecture. Now we must choose how to approach it. Again, we feel a sense of energy and openness. It is a time of development. As we test and refine multiple options, we again reach a point at which choices must be made. We kill our darlings, focus on what is possible and probable. It is time to deliver.

However, the 2004 Double Diamond is somewhat misleading. This is not quite how design, or sociolegal research, can ever work. A 2019 refresh sought to fill some gaps in the original,[1] but in my view, the resulting graphic is unclear. So I choose to focus on the original 2004 version, and note two absences, neither of which is fully resolved in the 2019 version, and both of which are relevant to the question of what designerly ways can do for sociolegal research.

First, the 2004 Double Diamond emphasizes the importance of experimentation primarily in the closed, scientific sense of 'testing', not in the open, 'makerly' (Akama et al. 2018, 106) sense of 'prising open' and '"following' (Ingold 2013, 7). It implies that design is a 'linear' and 'efficient' process, when in fact it is 'a messy journey, with much waste and looping backward'. And it buries the, equally messy, playful (Agamben and Fort 2007) role of abduction—the 'foggy… bit in the middle, which nobody can explain but which, coupled with a leap of faith, produces the spark for a compelling direction' (Winhall 2019). So it fails to capture the indeterminacy of design and designing and the importance of provisionality in design processes. These important characteristics are to some degree captured in Damien Newman's 'squiggle' (Figure 2.2), which represents design as beginning with a scramble of 'research and synthesis', characterized first by 'noise' and 'uncertainty', then by 'patterns' and 'insights', then calming into a more lolloping 'concept' and 'progression' phase, after which a single line of 'clarity' and 'focus' emerges and, finally, the 'design'.

Second, the 2004 Double Diamond focuses on the overall process and does not reference strategies. The container or ecosystem is presented as empty. So the graphic does not capture the visible, tangible communication strategies that are central to designerly ways; nor, therefore, the sociomaterial relationships that shape, are shaped by and give meaning to experimental processes and their outcomes.

A rough and ready visual solution might be to populate each side of the Double Diamond with squiggles, people, artefacts and so on. But the more

Figure 2.2 The process of design squiggle by Damien Newman, thedesignsquiggle
.com. Reproduced under CC-A-ND Works 3.0 United States License.

pressing task, to be addressed in the following sections, is to explain in
more detail how experimental processes and visible tangible communication strategies help to generate potentially enabling ecosystems and with
what risks and rewards, starting with some examples.

Examples of enabling ecosystems

As noted above, the 'ways' highlighted as 'designerly' in this volume run
fairly consistently across multiple fields of design. Here I will focus on how
they manifest in two subfields, Social Design and Policy Design, which
have particular resonance with sociolegal research, and that have already
shed important light on what designerly ways can do in social science
research contexts. To do this I will use two examples of existing practice:
The Fix and the ProtoPublics project.

Social design and policy design are especially relevant to sociolegal research for three reasons. First, they are generally focused more on
the communal and public, as opposed to individualistic or commercial,
spheres (see Julier 2017). Such designers are building on a long tradition—for example, the leaders of the German Bauhaus school of art and
design (1919-1933) began with the aim of designing things that were relevant, appealing, affordable, useful and even transformative to all, and
eventually came to see themselves as working for 'the harmonious arrangement of our society' (Saval 2019; Perry-Kessaris 2020). They tend to see
design as a communal resource, and are more likely to keep an eye on the
'longer-term consequences' and 'cumulative effects' of designs (Robinson
2019; see also Tonkinwise 2014, 7). Second, they are committed to helping

non-designers, who might include sociolegal researchers, to pursue their own interests in design mode. They seek to use their designerly expertise 'in a dialogic way ... to trigger', to 'support', but not to 'control' to generate potentially 'enabling ecosystems' (Manzini 2015, 65, 67 and 96–8 and 121). Third, processes and strategies from social design and policy design have already been deployed in a social science research context as part of the *ProtoPublics* project.

Social design brings communities together to address their shared challenges. Its more radical variants—such as social innovation, transformation and transition design—aim to 'generate answers that change the questions themselves' (Manzini 2015, 13–4); and in so doing to 'simultaneously meet social needs and create new social relationships or collaborations' that 'enhance society's capacity to act' in the future (Murray et al. 2010). By contrast, policy designers use service design techniques to improve the delivery of policy objectives by public authorities (see Bason 2014). They often work in the public innovation labs, the first of which to launch was Denmark's MindLab in 2002. These have become a common feature at every level of public administration and can be seen as part of wider trends towards evidence-based policy (Banerjee and Duflo 2010; World Bank 2015) and anticipation and experimentalism (Kimbell and Bailey 2017; Kimbell and Vesnić-Alujević 2020). A typical example is the UK Policy Lab, established in 2014 to prompt and facilitate civil servants to draw on design-based methods as part of a wider agenda to promote open, evidence-based policy making (Kimbell 2015; NESTA website). Its approach, set out in the Open Policy Making toolkit, includes experimental processes and visible and tangible communication strategies, and the various components are intended to be scalable, ready to be expanded or compressed into whatever time and resources are available—for example, it includes a section entitled 'What to do if you only have 24 hours' (Policy Lab 2016). As we shall see in the following sections, constraints are often seen as valuable and generative in design, and here Policy Lab is building on a format that emerged out of Google Ventures, known as a 'design sprint', which intentionally constrains time to promote innovative thinking (Knapp et al. 2016).

For a sense of what enabling ecosystems can look like in practice, we can look to The Fix—a radio programme that followed a multi-disciplinary team as they worked through a set of activities akin to the Policy Lab toolkit to generate solutions to social challenges, often within a single day sprint (BBC Radio Four 2017–2020).[2] I will focus on a set of three episodes from 2020 in which participants explored one theme, debt, over an extended period, and which, because the project involved close collaboration with private and public sector stakeholders, resulted in a fully tested pilot policy. The process began with the posing of a policy problem: Personal debt in an east London borough. First, there was a round of open, generative activity—empirical and empathy-building research in which the team familiarized themselves with the characteristics, perceptions, expectations and experiences of those associated with the problem, followed by a round of ideation in which each team member reframed the policy problem into a positive 'challenge', that is, one sentence, running to no more than four lines, beginning 'How can we...' written in thick black pen on A5 card. There was then a brief phase of closed, analytical editing. The team discussed the proposed challenges and decided which to focus upon. For example, 'How can we draw on capabilities and experience within the local community to support those in debt'. Next, there was a further phase of open, generative activity—empirical- and empathy-building research, drawing on data and engagement with specialists and users to help refine the wording of the chosen challenge, followed by another round of ideation to generate 'ideas that will answer the needs of users'. Initially, the emphasis was on quantity over quality; over time, weaker ideas—we might say, those that did not effectively meet the practical-critical-imaginative threshold—were discarded. The most promising ideas were pitched to the team, supported by lo-fidelity prototypes made of everyday materials such as paper and pipe-cleaners. For example, a broken washing machine was used to represent the fact that it is often a relatively small and foreseeable thing that pushes us into debt. No images are available from The Fix sprints, but a sense of what such prototyping typically looks like can be gleaned from Figure 2.1. Eventually, only a few 'well thought out ideas' remained. The idea that emerged from the Debt and Poverty sprint was 'I've been there'—a network of local residents with personal experience of debt, backed by a local public authority, to support those currently struggling. The basic components of the proposal were not necessarily entirely new, but they became more accessible, and their relevance clearer, within the enabling ecosystem of the sprint.[3]

Additional insights into what enabling ecosystems look like in practice can be found in the *ProtoPublics* research programme. In 2016, Lucy Kimbell, fresh from a year embedded with Policy Lab, and Guy Julier drew on their expertise in policy and social design approaches such as those outlined previously to lead the *ProtoPublics* research programme. Its aim was to 'clarify how a design-oriented approach complements and is distinct from other kinds of cross-disciplinary, co-produced research in relation to social issues'. A central element of the programme was the bringing together of five multi-disciplinary teams of social researchers in a sprint workshop during which each team co-designed a social science project. As part of that process, researchers engaged in collaborative, experimental processes in which they made their ideas visible and tangible in models. This emphasis on experimentation and 'collaborative "doing" and

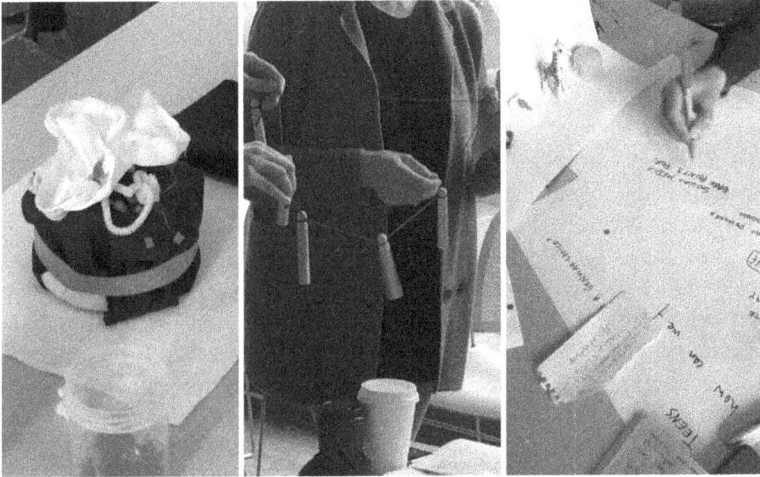

Figure 2.3 Scenes from prototyping phases during the 'Future Imaginaries' policy workshop organized by Lucy Kimbell at Central St Martins, 23 September 2016. Images: Amanda Perry-Kessaris.

"making" of the research' generated, in the terms of the present study, an enabling ecosystem. Within that ecosystem, participants 'from different backgrounds and with different capacities, many of whom previously did not know each other' found that they had an enhanced ability to communicate—'to share information and perspectives, generate ideas and engage in sense-making together'. Second, they found that mutual interpersonal trust was enhanced. As one participant put it: 'In previous projects I've taken trust for granted. In this one we didn't know each other and we had to create that trust in a very short time frame' (Julier and Kimbell 2016, 24). Third, they found that participants were better able to navigate between the actual and the potential. By creating 'visual outputs that foreground people's current experiences of a social issue' or 'mockups ... that project how things might be in the future' participants were able to 'instantiate in the present', digitally and/or materially, 'provisional aspects of the future' (Julier and Kimbell 2016, 41) (Figure 2.3).

Having gained a sense of how enabling ecosystems have been created in social and policy practice, and how they have been adapted to an academic context, we can now step back to consider the nuances of their core elements—experimentation, making things visible and tangible—across different contexts and timeframes.

Experimenting

Chapter 1 established that all forms of making are indeterminate, and must be approached provisionally, in a way that 'accommodate(s) both creative thinking and focus' (Norman 2004, 27). This requires a balance between direction and openness, decisiveness and ambiguity, culling and production: Structured freedom. Designers achieve and exploit the tension between structure and freedom through processes that promote experimentation, and they do this primarily by iteratively imposing and releasing constraints.

The introduction to the Double Diamond and sprinting focused on how design processes activate constraints around thinking, forcing us to switch between divergent and convergent modes. We can think of the divergent 'discovery' and 'development' phases of design processes as representing 'soft thinking' of the kind that we do when we are 'able to allow thoughts to bubble up and disperse freely, without nailing them down or only allowing in the ones that fits with a present framework' (James and Brookfield 2014, 14). They tend to be characterized by the phrase 'yes, and' (Stickdorn et al. 2018, 85), and to centre on the relatively abstract, imaginative, technique of ideation. And, as we shall see, this almost always involves making things visible and tangible—for example, using coloured sticky notes to place simple words and images in relation to each other on a wall in order to establish a 'common platform for communication' and a bespoke 'visual vocabulary' for the topic at hand. Especially when done collaboratively, ideation can 'brea[k] habits of perfectionism and ownership', encourage us to 'let go of' potentially 'obvious' ideas and 'make way for new', potentially 'more interesting, radical' ones (Stickdorn et al. 2018, 158 and 170–3). We can think of the convergent 'definition' and 'delivery' phases of the design process as representing 'hard thinking' that sees us 'decide to let go' (James and Brookfield 2014, 14). They tend to be characterized by the phrase 'yes, but' (Stickdorn et al. 2018, 85) and to rely on the relatively concrete, practical-critical technique of testing. Designers understand that good design rarely emerges from a 'wonderful, magical "divine spark"' (Dorst 2015, 40). So ideas are not 'especially valuable in themselves', they are merely potentially 'useful'. And rather than 'set out to find one killer idea as a starting point', they aim to produce them 'en masse' and then iteratively to deepen, diversify, cluster, blend, test, rank and champion them. In this way, they ensure that propositions have 'a firm foundation in reality' and/but that there is no need or expectation to 'ge[t] it right the first time'. Here, as we shall see, key characteristics of a proposed design are made visible and/or tangible in a digital or material model or draft (Stickdorn et al. 2018, 14, 92–3 and 157. See also Lupton 2011). Hard and soft modes of thinking are sometimes presented as incompatible, but experimental processes prompt and facilitate us to do both. The combined forces of divergence and convergence generate spaces that are at once safe and risky, open and closed, structured-yet-free. By prompting and facilitating us to, more or less systematically, open up and narrow down the range of issues and ideas under consideration, experimental design processes keep us moving and intentioned, focussed on the possibility of meaningful change.

Second, designers may activate constraints around scale. They break down 'problems into smaller bite-size pieces' or briefs to work backwards from a long-term goal via mid-term targets to near-future tasks (Cottam 2018, 235); and while some of these targets might be 'incremental', others will be 'disruptive' (Stickdorn et al. 2018, 11). Third, designers may activate constraints around time. In larger projects, they may generate 'an "ecology of times"', in which 'fast' experimental sprinting time can 'coexist' alongside 'slow' relational time (Manzini 2015, 25). Fourth, designers may activate constraints around space. They may search out spaces that fit the task at hand, they may adapt to whatever space is at hand or they may adapt a space to their needs. In these ways, they stimulate 'democratic participation, openness, play … and learning' all 'nested within' the structure of 'a specific context' and a 'specific' intended 'outcome' (Akama et al. 2018, 56).

A different balance between structure and freedom will be required depending on the context, especially the intention and the people (see Stikdorn et al. 2018, 368–75; Knap 2016). For example, Chapter 1 pointed to three opportunities that could be accessed through the provisional world of experimentation: Disruption, surrender and moving beyond. When the intention is to generate 'disruption', then relatively little structure is required to ensure that an experiment is meaningful. By contrast, the intention to prompt and facilitate participants to 'move beyond' requires a 'more closely convened and structured' environment—'a scaffolding', including, for example, a timetable, tasks and resources on which participants can 'stand' and a shared 'set of resources through which they might create possibilities'. And when the intention is to prompt and facilitate participants to 'surrender' then they must be 'highly constrained' through 'protocols' that are, for example, aimed at 'restricting time and movement' (Akama et al. 2018, 56 and 116). Turning to people, a 'creative' tag can be intimidating or off-putting, especially to lawyerly types. And when proposed in the absence of structured-yet-free mindsets and processes, such scepticism, even rejection, may be justified. Structure can help to mitigate the risk that we or others are not interested in, or lack confidence around, 'creativity'; or that we struggle to take it seriously as an intellectual exercise; or indeed that we are too diverted by the novelty of the 'creative' so that we lose track of our topic (see Lyon and Cabarellli 2016, 442).[4]

When we facilitate a collaborative experimental process we take on a complex 'status', sometimes 'master', sometimes 'servant'; and sometimes we will be willing and able to stay neutral as to substance, other times not. At all times we will be responsible for ensuring that participants feel 'safe' (Stickdorn et al. 2018a, 392–6), even if the aim of a particular activity is to unsettle. That which enables one person may, of course, disable another (see Mannay 2016, 87–95). There are steps that we can take to mitigate that risk—for example, we might emphasize the tangible over the visible when working with those whose vision is impaired; the digital over the material when travel is a problem; and the lo-fi over the luxurious when resources may be tight.[5] And, although we will not always be able to anticipate who might be excluded by our methodological choices, or to identify what adaptations will be most effectively mitigate that risk, there is no doubt that a proactively and explicitly inclusive orientation makes exclusion less probable. When we seek to create an enabling ecosystem that will endure, we need to take a 'processual approach' to inclusion, and to ethics more generally—to understand them as 'emergent from and part of' our process 'as it ongoingly develops' (Akama et al. 2018, 127). For example, in a series of workshops that they had deliberately laced with 'tension between looseness and tightness, … chance and expectation', Yoko Akama Sarah Pink and Shanti Sumartojo found that participants sometimes responded with 'frustration' and sometimes with 'enjoyment'—and 'both in extreme ways'. Some found the activities 'confusing', some would have preferred 'the purpose, benefits and outcomes of attending' to have been more fully 'explained' in advance, some simply 'left'. For Akama and colleagues, these responses were indicative not of success or defeat, but rather that their workshops had 'begun to dislodge some of the dominant rationales for why and how we do things', in particular, the notion that we are working in conditions of certainty and towards 'some predetermined outcomes.' But they acknowledge that there is a need to 'embed some controls'. At the same time, as the concept of design-after-design reminds us, whatever we design will be adapted by our users. So all we can do is to design in some 'parameters'—some structure—and embrace such use as participants make of what freedom remains (Akama et al. 2018, 32, 62–4, 67, 72–3 and 78).

Making

Many forms of design, such as graphic design, product design and fashion design, are explicitly and primarily about communicating things visibly and tangibly to end-users—in an app interface, in a car dashboard, in a uniform, in a visual contract. Indeed, all design is a form of rhetoric—'a persuasive argument that comes to life whenever a user considers or uses [it] as a means to some end' (Buchanan 1985). What I want to highlight here is that designers also make things visible and tangible as they go along. This allows them to generate, experience and investigate ideas differently—to see and touch, perhaps even to smell and taste them, to consider them separately and/or all at once and to move them around in relation to each other. This kind of visible and tangible making affords new ways of seeing and thinking; of collaborating and community building; and of communicating about what has been, what is and what might yet be.

... *to see*

Visual and material methods can prompt and facilitate us, as individuals and as members of a group, to see. Even if some of us cannot see or touch the artefact in which we have made our ideas visible or tangible, others can describe it, making it available to all. For example, service designers create journey maps to capture the sequence of steps through which a user will pass 'as a series of scenes, graphically annotated' with 'emotional' peaks and troughs of (dis)satisfaction relating to each 'touchpoint' between the actor and the other actors/factors involved in the experience, including definitive 'moments of truth'. All of this is overlaid with a 'dramatic arc' describing the level of 'engagement' of the key actor in the experience at any given moment, and regular instances of the question 'what if' to prompt consideration of possible problems. Similarly, designers make system maps to capture the components of a system that a user will come into contact with, but also capture the elements of their design process—as a 'sense-making' tool—that is, to gather together and synthesize their provisional conceptual language and disparate empirical data by representing them in images and text and placing them in relation to each other on a 'research wall' (Stickdorn 2018, 44–7, 56–8 and 128–9).

If we place representations of concepts, places and/or people in relation to each other in the same space, we may see connections and divergences hitherto overlooked, and 'amplify' relatively 'weak signals' that might otherwise be drowned out (Manzini 2015, 122–5; Woodward 2020, 153). When we externalize our ideas in a visible and tangible form, we generate a new space in which our ideas are made available to be explored, by ourselves and by or with others, from multiple 'positions, perspectives, levels of expertise, and understanding' (Malpass 2017, 62). We can interact directly with the idea and, because it has a material presence separate from its proponent, that interaction may be more probing, even forceful, without becoming awkward because we are exploring and testing the proposition, rather than its proponent.

... *to think*

We tend to understand reflection 'as a cognitive process'. But, in fact, we 'perceive' and, therefore, 'reflect with' all 'senses' in our 'embodied, mobile existence' (James and Brookfield 2014, 12–3). 'Looking at a photograph, listening to an interview, picking up and touching an object from the field' are ways in which we can 'resituate and recontextualise the data' (Woodward 2020, 140 and 143); or help us to, as they say, 'mak[e] the familiar strange, and the strange familiar' (see Manny 2016, 28). In such 'distantiation lies the possibility for a kind of reflexive self-awareness' in the sense that '[y]ou do not just see but you see yourself seeing' (Ingold 2013, 72). We may 'find our energy for the hard slog ... is renewed', and we are able to approach our work 'in new and unexpected ways', simply by asking 'the question "What would this look like if...?"' (James and Brookfield 2014, 5). So, since the early days of the Arts and Crafts Movement and the Bauhaus, designers have sought to communicate with themselves not only through physical engagement with artefacts but also through making as an embodied act (Weingarden 1985; Saletnik 2007; Perry-Kessaris 2020).

We all think 'through making' (Ingold 2013,126. See also Malpass 2016, 475). Ideas and artefacts are not 'buil[t] up from discrete', pre-selected 'parts' into a 'hierarchically organised totality'; nor does their final form necessarily reflect whatever the maker originally envisaged. Rather, they emerge from a 'process of growth', in which the maker is 'a participant in amongst a world of active materials' (Ingold 2013, 21, 39 and 45). And that process never reaches a complete and true ending because as artefacts are released into the wild, they are adapted, worn out and abandoned by users and happenstance (see Ahmed 2020).

Writing is a form of visible 'thinking through making'—that is, of thinking that 'goes along with, and continually answers to, the fluxes and floes of the materials', both abstract and concrete, 'with which we work' (Ingold 2013, 6), including our empirical data and disciplinary 'hinterland' (Law 2004). It happens iteratively over time and with multiple inputs. For example, when you edit an old sentence you are in conversation with yourself at another time. It is impossible to reconstruct edits, or the influence of conversations with ourselves and others, and it is rare for any given sentence to survive unscathed. But, while we may use brackets, highlights and strike-throughs to hold onto thoughts that are on their way in or out, we do not usually maintain a meaningful record of those comings and goings beyond hoarding old file versions (see Jacob 2017). Moreover, the passages of text that we work at are not especially amenable to agile experimentation. It can be hard to think differently with, or to let go of, a sentence or paragraph one it is written—each word anchored as it is between the prior and the next

When designers think through making, they do it visibly and tangibly. For example, architects 'typically sketch' when they are 'working out an idea'. Here sketching is 'a process of thinking' rather than 'the projection of a thought', and sketches themselves 'are *on their way* towards a proposition' (Ingold 2013, 126 and 128). As they become more certain, they begin to generate digital or material drafts of their idea—moving from, for example, two-dimensional sketches, to three-dimensional models, or animations. Individual elements of their drafts may be movable—for example, Post-it notes that can be gathered, stacked and reordered.

An important way in which designers think through making is prototyping. Prototypes can take almost any form, depending on the project at hand and the specific questions that they are intended to answer, and range in 'zoom level' from individual components to entire systems as well as in fidelity, from rough tabletop models made of cardboard to full-scale 'staged experiences' such as 'rehearsals, walkthroughs, simulations or pilots' using '[p]rops, actors and physical or digital models'. While '[d]irect experience' prototypes offer an embodied understanding of how it is to interact with a future object, process or system, 'indirect imagination' prototyping—that is, 'metaphorical simulations', such as role-play or sketches—generates an experience of 'think[ing] through, imagin[ing] or empathiz[ing]' around a future intended interaction (Stickdorn et al. 2018, 64, 227 and 231–43).

A designer's aim in communicating through prototypes may be primarily practical. To discover the 'possibilities and limitations of a design idea', to mitigate risks (Lim et al. 2008, 3), so that final designs are 'effective and meaningful' (Manzini 2015, 165. See also Strickdorn et al. 2018, 211; Burns et al. 2005, 23). Alternatively, a designer may prototype for critical purposes such as challenging and disrupting dominant perceptions and expectations, both within design and in the wider world, or for more imaginative purposes such as speculating around possible futures within design and in the wider world—to 'stimulate discourse around a topic by challenging the status quo' (Zimmerman et al. 2007, 497). For example, 'ambiguity' may be 'purposefully designed into' such artefacts in order to prompt and facilitate us to 'grappl[e] conceptually with objects, systems and their contexts', and thereby to generate 'deeper and more personal relations' in the issues being explored. Such artefacts are intended to be 'discursive' rather than 'explanatory'—to prompt and facilitate a 'diversification', as opposed to a 'simplification', of 'the ways in which we might understand' a given subject (Malpass 2016, 64 and 473–8).

'Prototypes are "'things that talk'" and that talk is generative (Corsín Jiménez 2014, 382. Quoting Lorraine Daston). They are 'powerful persuaders: you can go and visit, take part see and touch the new solution' and 'learn through doing'. They can prompt and facilitate us 'to suspend our current reality for just long enough for something else to emerge' (Cottam 2018, 224–5 and 236–7). And each new prototype 'encourages increasing complexity in the next' (Barton and James 2017, 252). This 'intrinsic futurity' can bring a sense of 'hopefulness and promise'. Prototypes are also 'inscriptive', in the sense that the knowledge and ideas that they generate are 'embodied in' them (Corsín Jiménez 2014, 382). They act as 'something to hold on to' as we 'transitio[n] from one way of thinking or behaving to another' (Cottam 2018, 236). Because they at once generate and inscribe ideas, prototypes capture a combination of pasts, presents and futures. They are both 'actual and potential' (Julier and Kimbell 2016, 39). And by emphasizing, rather than resolving, that which is provisional within a design, while at the same time maintaining a practical focus on the specifics of a design challenge, prototypes promote innovation—that is, meaningful contribution (Kimbell 2019).

... to collaborate

One of our most important and difficult tasks as researchers is to ensure that we transition from the kind of thinking-writing that we must do to formulate and express our own ideas to ourselves, to the kind of user-centred communication that we must offer up if we are to have a hope of changing how others think or behave (McEnerney 2014)—that is, to make a meaningful research contribution. If we practise communicating our ideas visibly and tangibly along the way, we will be better placed to make our plain text communications more meaningful—accessible, engaging, relevant—not least by avoiding jargon (Cottam 2018, 239; Mazé and Redstrom 2007; Manzini 2015, 125).

Making ideas visible and tangible can prompt and facilitate us to translate ideas across divides. When we have something in common to look at or touch, we may be able to 'understand each other better' (Stickdorn 2018, 42–3). We may form a 'common language' (Cottam 2018, 227) through which to surface and develop shared ideas. Susan Leigh Star (1989) introduced the concept of 'boundary objects' to explain one mechanism by which such translation occurs. For example, a case study of a Californian zoological museum collection found that a diverse group of collaborators—administrators, sponsors, curators, theorists, amateurs—relied on a particular array of concrete things and abstract theories to 'translat[e] between viewpoints', and 'maintai[n] coherence' across disciplinary and professional divides. These 'objects' existed, abstractly and/or concretely, at the 'boundaries' of the worlds inhabited by the collaborators. Their exact meaning and function varied across these 'social worlds', but 'their structure' was 'robust' and 'common enough to ... make them recognizable' across, and therefore to act as 'means of translation' between, these worlds (Star and Griesemer 1989, 393 and 408). These boundary objects opened the door to 'generalizable findings' while honouring 'divergent viewpoints' (Star and Griesemer 1989, 408).

What designers do that is distinctive is to gather concrete boundary objects together, and to render abstract 'boundary objects' concrete in Post-it notes, sketches, photographs, models and so on (see Stickdorn 2018, 43; Rhinow et al. 2012, 2-10). For example, journey maps and system maps are boundary objects. In a collaborative and participatory context they may both journey maps and system maps may 'facilitate a common understanding' by enabling different actors such as research participants, users and stakeholders/publics to 'work together efficiently and creatively with' a particular experience as the 'common denominator' (Stickdorn 2018, 46).

Artefacts arising from such exercises can form part of a 'tactic of articulation' in which 'objects, people, and actions' are linked together to form 'an agonistic collective—an open space of contest in which the elements gathered together are able to act out a plurality of conflicting practices, values and beliefs'. A 'public' is being 'constructed around' the idea (DiSalvo 2012, 94). For example, we might think of researchers as developing into co-design 'networks' in which '[m]ore or less strong, dense, stable relationships [are] formed', and in which research/co-design is a type of 'social conversation' (Manzini 2015, 48–9). The result may not be consensus, and consensus may well not be the aim. It is possible, for example, to co-make with 'one pen' on 'one page', with 'many pens' on 'one page' or with 'many pens' on 'many pages' (Stickdorn et al. 2018, 407–15). What is likely to result, and what is necessary, is a greater sense of coherence in that co-makers will better see and understand the nature and significance of any diversity in their understandings of the topic at hand (Star and Griesemer 1989, 388).

… *to build community*

Designers tend to emphasize iterative 'doing', rather than 'talking', and this can prompt and facilitate inclusive collaboration (Stickdorn et al. 2018, 415). For example, designers are inclined to understand from the very word 'workshop' that the 'purpose' will be 'learning through hands-on-doing'— that is, 'work' in a 'shop' or space—and to appreciate the workshop as 'a site of intervention … an opening up of possibilities'. Whether working alone or in groups, they tend 'to share, experience, imagine or problem-solve an issue through intensive teamwork'. They may 'invoke' the 'qualities' of communal makerspaces by engaging in 'a series of staged activities' centred on 'playful' and 'generative forms of material making'; and drawing on 'the idea of sensemaking—making sense of what we do together'. For example, rather than holding a 'book launch', Akama and colleagues designed a book 'landing'—that is, a participatory workshop in which readers were invited to remake copies of the book in ways that threw back themes of uncertainty and possibility to the organizers (2018, 12 and 64. Emphasis removed). And they may activate the power of place-making—the knowledge that a place is 'a space' that is made 'meaningful' or 'endowed with sense' through the interactions of those who are using or have used it (Manzini 2015, 189).

Indeed, the co-making of ideas in a visible and tangible form can go well beyond the creation of shared visual, material and conceptual spaces. It can be seen as a 'direct' act of community building (Manzini 2015, 174 and 122) in the sense that it is both reliant on and generative of mutual interpersonal trust. Participating in communities, whether 'on the fringes' or 'at the heart' is 'a complex process that combines doing, talking, thinking, feeling and belonging. It involves our whole person, including our bodies, minds, emotions and social relations', and is often 'evoked in material objects that symbolize the identity, ethos and values of the community that produced them' (James and Brookfield 2014, 186–7. Quoting Wenger 1998). This is why we create logos, programmes, lanyards and websites. We could do so much more. It is not by chance that communication and community share the Latin root *communis* meaning common, public, general, shared by all or many. For example, Akama and colleagues use Donna Harraway's concept of 'becoming with' to signal a 'commitment' among event participants 'to travel along together', in the spirit of companionship (Akama et al. 2018, 62). Of course, visual methods do not necessarily resolve 'issues of power and positionality'. An ostensibly collaborative visualization may simply express the views of dominant group members (Mannay 2016, 46–7 and 52), and there is always a risk that visual and material strategies may encourage us 'only' to 'recognize change' when it is 'visible and vocal' (Akama et al. 2018, 132).

The ability to gather, especially physically, is a luxury that we ought not to waste. It requires resources—ecological, financial, technological, physical, emotional, temporal. And, as those constrained by limited resources, inaccessible facilities, caring responsibilities and visa refusal have long known, but perhaps the pandemic that took global hold in 2020 has begun to bring more starkly home to all, our ability to assemble can be taken away—and with it all manner of generative happenstance and serendipity. We ought to take this opportunity to think more about how, why and where we assemble, whether virtually or face to face. Despite our social understanding of law, we sociolegal researchers tend towards the individualistic—my ideas, my presentation, my paper, my citations. We do not generate structures to hold each other together, nor, therefore, do we do much to generate a sense of freedom. In planning sociolegal events, our biggest 'design' decisions tend to revolve around the titles of papers, and the composition of panels; and most knowledge generation will occur through the individual preparations of the presenters and in the note-taking of audience members. Both in our capacities as organizers and in our capacities as participants, we quash our uncertainty around what success might look like, and whether we will achieve it and, likely impaired by some combination of anxiety and hubris, we carry on, operating more in parallel or in series than in communion. There are limits to how far all of this can take us towards the goals of making meaningful contributions and engaging in meaningful research relations. For example, we need to pay more attention to the fact that gathering allows us to go beyond the exchange of ideas, to begin to co-create them and to focus on how we can convert our assemblies into sites of empirical investigation and knowledge generation—to 'commit to the idea that knowing is not only situated in disciplines, and that knowing is emergent from … encounters' (Akama et al. 2018, 20). And this requires that we attend to each phase—before, during and after of those assemblies; and to all kinds of participants—including all their potentially constrained physical, cognitive and emotional capacities.

Caveats

We can do more to design potentially enabling ecosystems for ourselves as individuals and as groups in our research projects and events. The remainder of this book gives examples, drawn from expert and non-expert design practice, of how experimental processes can prompt and facilitate us to progress provisionally; how we can make ideas, actors, values, quantities, connections, sentiments and so on visible and tangible at any and all of the mutually constitutive phases of our sociolegal research—conceptualization, data gathering, analysis, communication and reflection—and how all of this can enhance our ability to engage in meaningful research relations and make meaningful research contributions.

But design is not magic. It is wonderfully horribly human. Like law, and like sociolegal research, design can embed and reproduce exclusionary ideologies—racism, sexism, ableism, classism and so on (Boehnert and Onafuwa 2016, 5. See also Yashaswi 2019; Pater 2016)—with potentially lethal consequences (Criado Perez 2020).[6] And it too can make us resistant to multiplicity and change. Indeed, Arturo Escobar sees contemporary mainstream design as an extension of the 'universalizing', Eurocentric, 'ontology of dominant forms of modernity', which not only shapes our unequal presents but can also 'eliminate possible futures' (2017, 16 and 66); Anne-Marie Willis suggests that '[c]onventional discipline-based design education cannot contribute to substantial change unless students are inducted into understanding theories of power, social structure and social change, and the like' (2015, 74); and Tim Brown argues that design 'has become too important to be left to designers' (2009, 8). The purposes for which it is deployed can be very bad indeed. And however 'good' their intentions, designers sometimes fail to include and to enable. Sometimes designers forget certain user groups entirely;[7] sometimes they design to their own needs, assuming that they match those of users. For example, nondisabled human-computer interaction designers have been criticized for using 'empathy-building activities'—for example, observing people who have disabilities or engaging in the 'temporary simulation of bodily impairments'—rather than engaging those who have disabilities as co-designers (Bennett and Rosner 2019, 2–3. See also Kafer 2013). Sometimes design offers no more than gloss—'tricks and techniques'—which may feel 'liberating and inspiring' but do not give us what 'we really need' (Dorst 2015, 2). Sometimes designers suffer from a 'saviour' complex (Irani 2018), believing that they have 'superior training and ethical tools to quickly assess and innovate on problems in domains they are unfamiliar with' (Bennett and Rosner 2019, 3). Sometimes they fix on producing change regardless of whether it is needed (Norman 2010). Indeed, an appreciation for the idea that 'Whatever the question, design has an answer' (Design Council website. See also Burns et al. 2005, 9) is to some extent 'institutionalized in professional education programs', 'encoded in workbooks and guides' and 'popularized' by influential bodies such as design firm IDEO (Irani 2018, 2–3). In its more aggressive 'design thinking' or 'saviour' incarnations, design can become 'kind of like syphilis—it's contagious and rots your brains' (Vinsel 2017. See also Schwab 2018).

So, I am not debating whether designers are more successful than sociolegal researchers at, for example, including and enabling, or making contributions that will be meaningful. I am proposing that design offers ways that might enhance the ability of sociolegal researchers to do better. As designers and social scientists are each drawn ever further into the other's sphere of competence in academia (Mazé 2016, 50) and in the wider world (Corsín Jiménez 2014), the need for cross-disciplinary training and collaboration becomes ever more pressing. We need to keep each other honest. In that spirit, this chapter ends with an emphasis on the need for sociolegal researchers to acquire a degree of visual and material literacy.

Many visual and material methods require technical skills that most sociolegal researchers will never achieve, and Chapter 4 underlines that message by introducing the work of a selection of sociolegally-attuned expert designers. A core message of this volume, not least the tasks set out in Chapter Five, is that there is much to be gained from non-experts engaging in low-tech making. But it is important to highlight the risks associated with non-expert low-tech dabbling in the visual and material, not least since sociolegal 'turns' towards the visual and the material have not always been as well-informed or systematic—visually and materially literate—as they have been enthusiastic (Mulcahy 2017, S112–S114 and S128. See also Woodward 2020, 3–4).

To be visually literate is to be 'able to read and write' visual or material language including the ability 'to decode (interpret)' and to 'encode (compose)' messages (Ausburn and Ausburn 1978b). Every language consists of 'vocabulary, grammar and syntax' of 'culturally acquired signs' that are 'intentionally use[d]' in 'culturally acquired patterns' to communicate meaning. And every visual language is communicated through a medium— for example, we might communicate through our bodily movements, such as gesture; through objects, such as sculptures; through sign and symbols such as emojis; or through the abstract graphic language of colour, juxtaposition, scale, space, shadow, perspective and so on (Avgerinou and Ericson 1997, 285). Verbal languages communicate meaning through both denotation—that is, the precise definition of a word such as one might find in a dictionary—and connotation—that is, the wider emotions and imagery associated with the word. By contrast, visual and material languages only operate at the level of connotation (Mannay 2016, 64 and 74). Because literacy is contextual, and needed of both the sender and recipient, any form of communication across social worlds is a delicate matter. For example, both attitudes to colour and the meanings ascribed to specific colours vary greatly across time and space (St Clair 2016, 29–30); there is 'significant potential for miscommunication' even among that most ubiquitous of visual languages, emojis (Miller et al. 2016); and there is no fixed 'relationship between material properties and intended meanings' (Karana et al. 2010, 292) nor 'between what we see and what we know' (Berger 1972, 1). So we usually need some verbal or textual narration to 'anchor' an image or artefact in the intended meaning, and here we must draw on relevant cultural contexts (see Rose 2016, Chapter 6; Crow 2003). If we want to produce or repurpose visuals and materials to communicate a particular, anchored, meaning—for example, a visualization representing quantitative data we have collected, then we will need to acquire a degree of literacy and technical skills. Chapter 5 includes some points of departure.

If, on the other hand, we are generating or selecting materials/visuals as inspiration, or as part of a thinking-through-making process, then visual and material literacy are less relevant. However, we should remain alert to the fact that visual and material sources can produce effects that go beyond aesthetics and functionality: Their effects can be performative. To paraphrase Willis (2006) once more, we design the world, and our world designs us back. We ought, for example, to heed the cautionary tale presented by economics where 'a handful of diagrams' so powerfully 'frames' economic thinking that '[i]f we want to write a new economic story we must draw new pictures' (Raworth 2017, 24. See also Williams 2019, 232). And where trust is low, and/or there is uncertainty about the authenticity of a message that we are trying to interpret, communication is further impeded (Latour 2002, 20): 'We love the image and we hate it. We are enchanted by its vivid persuasive power but remain fearful of being seduced and deceived' (Sherwin 2011, 5 and 173–4).[8] Furthermore, we will need to consider how to secure the post-project life of any visual and material data generated as part of a project in ways that will be meaningful to others (Pauwels 2010, 560–56; Mannay 2016, 87 and 102–4). While each individual visual or material artefact may be capable of communicating something, 'it is in their hybridity' and as an assemblage that they 'make sense' (Julier and Kimbell 2016, 54). The question of what to do with it all is of concern not only to researchers but also, for example, to publishers and librarians.

If we intend to interpret the meaning of visual or material artefacts produced by another—for example, analyzing a painting for its 'internal organisation … and the salience of the multiple contexts in which [it] is seen felt and interpreted' in a way that goes behind, to use Barthe's term, the immediate 'punctum' or emotional impact of an artefact (Mannay 2016, 79), then we are moving beyond doing sociolegal research in design mode. Here we need to engage with expert visual and material analytical frameworks such as iconology, or other theoretical frameworks such as semiotics, rhetoric, psychoanalysis, cultural studies, postcolonial theory and feminist theory, as adapted for visual and material analysis (Pauwels 2010, 560. See Berger 1972; Rose 2016) and adapted once more for application in legal spheres (see, for example, Goodrich 2015).

Finally, it is worth noting that there will be ethical risks associated with the production, use and storage of any visuals/materials generated through participatory research that extend well beyond the need to obtain consent from those who appear in photos or videos. For example:

> where topics are particularly sensitive and where visual images act to present, and fix, participants for 'time immemorial', researchers need to think carefully about whether this recognition is ethical, both in the moment and beyond the lifetime of the study.
>
> (Mannay 2016, 114–6)

Notes

1 For example, it includes the idea that 'no idea is ever finished'—that designs are the subject of continuous iterative feedback loops shaped by social relations

of leadership, user-engagement, collaboration and co-creation (Design Council 2019).

2 See also case studies described by Lucy Kimbell (2015) in her report detailing a year spent embedded with Policy Lab during its first year of operation.

3 The council leader indicated during the programme that the idea would be implemented, and possibly extended to apply to other issues such as knife crime, however, at the time of writing, there is no sign on the council website of any such implementation—perhaps because of the pandemic, perhaps because change is hard.

4 This is a problem inherent to sociolegal and other interdisciplinary forms of research, and in some ways, the presence of visible tangible artefacts, and the opportunity to point and ask, for example, 'where is law?', can make it easier to address.

5 For example, in designing artefacts for the Sociolegal Model-Making project, available at amandaperrykessaris.org, I chose a combination of lo-fi formats, inspired in part by Ruben Pater's (2013) Drone Survival Guide to work against the centralized quality of standard sociolegal publications, and luxury formats to gesture towards what might be possible with resources.

6 The Design Council reported 'the UK's design workforce' was 22 per cent female (versus 51 per cent of the general population), falling to 17 per cent at management level. However, it was more ethnically representative with 13 per cent being of 'Black, Asian and other minority ethnic' background (versus about 16 per cent of the general UK population as recorded in the 2011 census), falling to 12 per cent at management level (2018, 14). No data was published regarding disability.

7 Sometimes designers cannot see, or are not allowed to take account of, certain users or third parties whose interests may be implicated by a design. For example, Linda Mulcahy (2011) has shown how the *Court and Tribunal Design Guide* impacts negatively on defendants, who, in the 2019 iteration of the Guide, are not even identified as 'users' (see Mulcahy and Rowden 2019).

8 We want, in the words of Judith Butler, to 'break the frame' placed around the communication by those who may seek to control its effect (Mannay 2016, 79).

3 Working in design mode

This chapter demonstrates what it can mean to do sociolegal research in design mode using examples from my own practice. Here I am placing myself as an experienced non-expert designer, as distinct from the experienced experts introduced in Chapter 4, and from the inexperienced and non-expert potential designers within the sociolegal research community to whom this monograph is primarily directed. The following examples use processes that promote experimentation and visible tangible communication strategies to generate a proto-enabling ecosystem whether for an individual researcher, groups of researchers or researchers and their informants and participants. Each example is itself a material, ethnographic experiment—a way of testing and exploring what it might mean to do sociolegal research in design mode as an individual or as a group, and what might be the risks and rewards.[1] And each example represents, evidences and deepens arguments laid in Chapters 1 and 2 as to the sociolegal relevance of designerly ways.

The following sections first introduce a typology of modes making as an accessible frame through which sociolegal researchers can better understand and further develop what it might mean to do research in design mode. It then explains how I have used them—whether in isolation, in parallel or in series—using examples drawn from research fieldwork and research events.

Modes of making

In the course of my experimentation at the intersections of sociolegal research and design, I developed a typology of modes of making—modular, found and bespoke—which I disseminated through a downloadable collection of designed artefacts as part of the Sociolegal Model-Making project.[2] Although those artefacts were specifically intended to prompt and facilitate sociolegal researchers to engage in model-making, it is an accessible vantage

DOI: 10.4324/9780367177683-3

point from which to consider making more generally. Each mode of making can prompt and facilitate us to activate our practical sense, so that we can better explain what and how; our critical sense so that we can better ask why; and our imaginative sense so that we can better speculate about 'what if' and behave prefiguratively 'as if'. Each mode can be used in any phase of the sociolegal research process, and the emphasis may be on the empirical or conceptual worlds that are the focus of the research, the research project or process and/or on the researcher. As we shall see, we can combine individual instances of making to form a larger process or event—for example, through multiple engagements with one mode of making, or by engaging in a series of multiple modes of making, and the results of the mode of making can be brought together as an assemblage, by one researcher or many, for exhibition. The resulting artefacts can be understood as 'metaphorical and symbolic' representations of 'problems, solutions' and 'realizations', as opposed to the kind of 'literal models' used by architects (James and Brookfield 2014, 116). Just like the abstract models beloved of economists, they 'capture the most relevant aspect of reality in a given context' so that it becomes possible to 'show how specific mechanisms work by isolating them from other, confounding effects'. So the fact that they do not reflect all 'facets of the real world' is 'a feature, not a bug' (Rodrik 2016, 11–3. Emphasis removed).

Modular

In 'modular' mode we make ideas visible and tangible using a pre-fabricated set of components such as sticky notes on a wall, index cards or building blocks on a table. Some modular systems, such as sticky notes, are designed for the kind of strategic thinking and action associated with management; others, such as LEGO, are designed to be playful. But the distinction is not significant in practice: Play is increasingly seen as a powerful force for personal and wider social change (Kane 2004); and the LEGO Group has designed and commercialized a decision-making system built around the idea of non-'trivial' play, or play with intention, to support long-term planning in commercial and non-commercial settings (James and Brookfield 2014, 62 and 115–6. See also Peabody and Noyes 2017; Woodward 2020, 72). Modular systems present a relatively smooth entry point into making things visible and tangible because they offer a ready-made visual vocabulary and, therefore, immediate results and because they are scalable in terms of size, complexity and sophistication. As such, they seem to reduce anxiety around the idea of being creative and associated agonizing over getting everything right from the outset. However, attention has been drawn to the risks that their inherent linearity and commercial associations may stifle creativity (Page and Gundersen 2016; Mannay 2016, 71; Perry-Kessaris 2016c).

When I have engaged sociolegal researchers in modular making, whether individually or in gatherings of up to 100, they have reported, for example, that it has allowed them to 'see the connections' between different aspects of their project and to identify 'where the connection was actually not that strong'; to learn about and understand the work of fellow researchers; to focus on aspects of research 'that have been missing so far'; to 'reflect on alternative solutions'; 'to express relatively unformed ideas'; to 'sit back and analyse' what they have made and thereby engage in 'reflexive insight'; 'instinctually' to 'add elements' and only 'later ... to see how they fit' with the conceptual frame of the project; and to realize 'that we should discuss our projects more, to learn more from each other' (see Chapter 5).[3]

Found

In 'found' mode, we make ideas visible and tangible using something that we have come across such as an artefact in a museum, shells on a beach or photos returned in an online keyword search. Found making promotes more divergent, generative, thinking than modular making. But our attention is focused—converging—upon whatever we have found. It is a prompt. For example, through her analysis of the use by the General Medical Council of the 'strikethrough' to indicate the removal of a doctor from the register of medics, Marie-Andrée Jacob has exposed how 'found objects, even the most technical, can be turned into analytical devices and used as a "way in" to think about problems' (Jacob 2017, 140). In this way, we can 'take advantage' of the 'huge data repositories of actual, historic, and fictional(ized) worlds' that are continuously created in the course of both everyday and expert (inter)actions (Pauwels 2010, 550). We may be drawn to a thing because it is directly, concretely involved in some aspect of our research, because it resembles some aspect of the research or because it is an indirect symbol of some aspect of our research (see Woodward 2020, 150). When I have engaged sociolegal researchers in found model-making, as described in the 'Pop-up museum of legal objects projects' section, they have reflected, for example, that the process of choosing an object 'opened up avenues I had not considered for conceptualising the role of law' and that is was 'really productive ... freed me to interrogate and expand my own assumptions'.

Bespoke

In 'bespoke' mode we make ideas visible and tangible from scratch using basic ingredients –for example, modelling clay, cardboard, ink, pencil, glue and/or string—to make an artefact that is intended to represent one or more aspects of the research such as a person or concept. Because it entails making something entirely new, it promotes relatively divergent thinking and is especially well suited to imaginative thinking, including future-focused speculation and prefiguration (see Chapter 4).

Depending on the materials that we use, the process of making is more or less likely to activate our 'sensory awareness' as well 'the generative currents' of the materials with which we are making (Ingold 2013, 7 and 73). Through more 'embodied making', we can bring together the reflective, behavioural and visceral levels of processing in 'a unity of cognitive and bodily processes' (Gulliksen et al. 2016, 1; Norman 2004, 22). Bodies are, like materials, something to think from as well as about. '[W]e do not … experience ourselves and one another as "packaged" but as moving and moved—that is, in *correspondence*—with the things around us'. Bodies are, like materials, something to think from as well as about (Ingold 2013, 94). Later we can use what we have made to think further. We can hold the chosen 'aspect' of the research project, materialized in a drawing or a model, in our hand and in our mind, in the office and in the field. Indeed, poet Roger Robinson writes of hiding 'a portable paradise' in your pocket: '[I]f life puts you under pressure', you can secretly 'trace its ridges' or, better still, 'empty your paradise onto a desk … shine the lamp on it like the fresh hope of morning, and keep staring at it till you sleep' (Robinson 2019, 81). In feedback on the 'Making things visible and tangible' workshop, which is detailed in a forthcoming section, participant Luke McDonagh reported:

> At the time, I did not think much of the bespoke modelling—fun as it was … However, I have cooked my models and keep them on my desk, and—when admin and teaching loads permit—I pick them up and reflect and process my research. They are handy (literally) for externalising thoughts, for reflecting on what I am doing and where I am going, and reminders of my focus. I think they will, in the long run, be the most useful, even though at the time of making them I was not sure of their value.

Modelling island-wide economic life in Cyprus

This section focuses on three instances in which I have operated in design mode as part of my ongoing research into actual-potential island-wide economic life on the island of Cyprus in the Eastern Mediterranean. Divisions between Greek Cypriots and Turkish Cypriots grew under the British in the 1950s, deepened around independence and exploded in 1974 with an attempted Greek-backed coup, followed by military occupation of the north by Turkey, the mass displacement of civilians, the emergence of the predominantly unrecognized Turkish Republic of Northern Cyprus in 1983 and a general suspension of island-wide interactions. Hopes of reconciliation were raised in 2003 when the north opened crossing points and in 2004 when the island joined the European Union, but UN-sponsored talks have since failed to generate a solution. Today, the island is in an in-between state—neither at war nor at peace, neither whole nor fully split—which constrains life at every level (Hatay et al. 2008). But there have always been Cypriots in the public, private and civil society sectors who have speculatively asked 'what if' the island were not divided, and those who have gone further, acting prefiguratively, 'as if' there were an integrated island-wide economy (see Chapter 4). And the possibility remains open that such an economy might emerge once more.

As we shall see in Chapter 4, we can draw on architect Eyal Weizman (2017, 65–6) to think of sociolegal research as operating across three 'sites': The 'field' where the life of law is lived and from which we gather signs of that life, the 'studio' where we analyse what signs of life we have gathered and composed into arguments and the 'forum' where those arguments are presented and challenged. The following sections show how my material metaphoricization and model-making have allowed me to more easily translate and sustain ideas across different 'sites' or my research in Cyprus—to simultaneously keep in mind, for example, the concrete people and abstract concepts that are relevant to my research, and the geographical spaces to which they relate; and, at the same time, to imagine alternatives.

Material metaphoricization

We humans 'live by' metaphors. '[T]he essence of metaphor is understanding and experiencing one kind of thing in terms of another'. There are very few aspects of our lives that are clear and discrete enough that we are able to see, understand and speak about in direct terms; and we conceptualize the rest of our lives in, with reference to, those terms (Lakoff and Johnson 1980, 143). So a metaphor draws its meaning, 'coherence and persuasiveness' from the social context within which it arises (Winter 2007, 872). In addition to doing the practical, structured, work of helping to communicate and fixing our meaning, metaphors can also do the imaginative, free, generative work of helping us to see or understand things differently (Winter 2007, 897).

A metaphor may be communicated textually, in a single word or parable (James and Brookfield 2014 p 110); abstractly, in a theoretical model; visually, in a still or moving image; and/or materially, in materials, objects or things. Textual metaphoricization pervades legal discourse. For example, we speak of 'high and low courts', the need to 'balance and weigh interests' and the 'carrying of a right or an obligation' (Philippopoulos-Mihalopoulos 2016, 56 and 60). I had the opportunity to explore the potential of material metaphoricization as part of a project completed with fellow design student Andy Renmei in which we interviewed Zoe Laughlin, an artist, maker and materials engineer who is co-founder and co-director of the Institute of Making at University College London.

The Institute is home to a Materials Library—'a growing repository of some of the most extraordinary materials on earth, gathered together for their ability to fire the imagination and advance conceptualisation' (Institute of Making website). We wanted to understand how a materials-based gaze might 'fire imagination and advance conceptualisation' in relation to the theme of social transformation—for example, the kinds of social transformations that shape Cypriot pasts, presents and futures. So we selected four items that are categorized by the Library as 'transformative': Muscle wire, bioactive glass scaffold, ferrofluid and self-healing concrete. We anticipated that we might be able to use their capacity for transformation as material metaphors of social transformation, and we asked Zoe Laughlin to 'perform' them for us. For example, she showed us how muscle wire, which had been pre-formed at a high temperature into the shape of a paperclip, could be repeatedly bent out of shape by hand and restored to the paper clip shape with the application of heat (Figure 3.1). In her words:

Figure 3.1 Zoe Laughlin introduces materials on the theme of transformation at the UCL Institute of Making. Images: Amanda Perry-Kessaris and Andy Renmei, 2016.

This is often described as a shape memory alloy because it has this ability to remember shape. But it also has ability to have its memory change and to lose its memory. Because over time it will fatigue and the material with wear out and the crystals won't spring back quite as exuberantly as they once did. ... It will tire and it will lose that memory. But also you can change its memory by essentially 'annealing' it—bringing the metal close up to the melting point and then the crystals will realign themselves and that will be their new set position.

(Perry-Kessaris and Renmei 2016)

To my sociolegal gaze, the muscle wire offered a compelling material metaphor for social habits—specifically, the idea that law can pull people away from their habits, but that those habits are often resilient, so we may return to them in spite of the law, but that after a time those habits may be broken.

Another material performed by Laughlin was bioactive glass—a porous, brittle compound that is intended to be implanted between fragments of bone inside the human body and to serve as a 'scaffold' upon which new own-grown bone can develop, and which then eventually dissolves away. I chose to reinterpret the physical properties of bioactive glass scaffold as the properties of law and legal systems; the human body as social life; and the processes by which the glass scaffold is integrated into the human body as social change and the internalization of norms. And I have found the language and insights that I developed in the process to be useful in thinking about the potential risks and rewards of external intervention in changing attitudes around law and island-wide economic life (see Perry-Kessaris 2016d).

Through these 'performances' of materials, Laughlin demonstrated her assertion that, by engaging with materials, you can 'advance your ability to think. It can change your ability to conceptualize because you now understand something about the world, differently, and now you've got a new way of imagining things' (Perry-Kessaris and Renmei 2016).

Developing a space and a language for uncomfortable and sensitive topics

Researching interactions between predominantly Greek Cypriot southerners and predominantly Turkish Cypriot northerners on the famously 'divided' island of Cyprus is difficult because such life was for many years, and is in many respects, 'illegal'; and because it continues to be deeply sensitive and relatively rare (Papadakis et al. 2006). Island-wide economic life is sometimes viewed with a particular disdain. In order to address these constraints, I have developed a model-making strategy that can be thought of as pre-figurative (see Chapter 4). It is designed to prompt and facilitate me and my interlocutors to act 'as if' there already exists an environment conducive to researching this topic, in particular, by allowing us to develop a visual, and then verbal, language for communicating across multiple divides about the concepts, actors and relationships at the heart of my research.

It was important to root myself as much as possible in Cyprus, but at the same time, to step outside of the rigid, and in overwhelmingly hope-less, often ethno-nationalistic dominant framings of the contemporary 'Cyprus Problem'. So I began with artefacts that I 'found' among the artefacts and interpretive materials in around 25 museums across the island, as well as in the British Museum in London. Just as museums use their 'collections, exhibitions, objects and interpretive material as a way of selectively con-structing collective memories' (Stylianou-Lambert and Bounia 2016), so I wanted to use those collections to construct an open research space. I selected a full-scale ox-hide copper ingot exhibited at the British Museum as well as miniature 'votive' versions of such ingots exhibited in the Cyprus Museum in Nicosia and used them to think through key concepts such as burial, memory, transformation, networking and hope (Perry-Kessaris 2017a, 240–3). I selected terracotta figures dating from 1900 BCE exhib-ited at the Cyprus Museum, and used them to think about key actors in my research—namely, those wishing to engage in island-wide economic life—and I selected a ship (750–475 BCE) from Limassol Archaeological Museum to represent the shared future-focus that can be implied by eco-nomic interactions. Then I made my own 'bespoke' clay representations of those artefacts. Some of that making was done individually and some was done collaboratively with my children when each was aged around 12 years, in order to further test the communicative potential of this strategy. As we made the figures, we discussed the origins and significance of the artefacts, as well as the ideas that we intended them to represent. Finally, I designed several material spaces—printed vinyl mats—to represent the sociolegal field of island-wide economic life, into which I could place the clay representations and begin to think about law as not only preventing but also facilitating, and maybe even generating new spaces for, island-wide economic life (Figure 3.2).

Over a period of years, I have taken these artefacts to locations—ancient and modern, urban and rural, coastal and inland, northern, southern and in between—some of which are relevant to, or having resonance with, island-wide economic life, others not at all. There I have used the artefacts to speculate about possible futures for island-wide and intercommunal eco-nomic life in Cyprus, as well as to test out different ways of presenting my argument. I documented those experiments in photographs, videos and blogs, as well as in more formal films (see Perry-Kessaris 2016e).[4] Over time I have developed a vocabulary for communicating about this topic

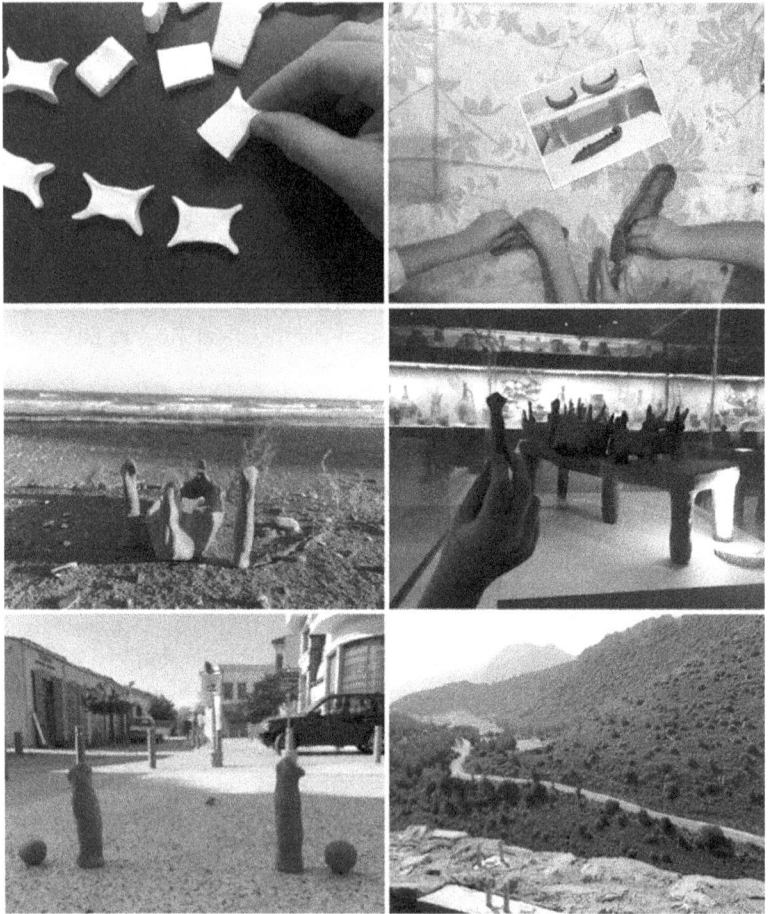

Figure 3.2 Making clay replicas of ancient museum artefacts and placing them in locations across the island. Images: Amanda Perry-Kessaris.

with myself—a researcher feeling her way through a complex and sensitive topic—with non-expert collaborators, and with diverse expert interlocutors such as legal practitioners, economic experts and local, foreign and international bureaucrats and activists. I have introduced the artefacts into interviews where I have used them to narrate, test and refine my current thinking and outstanding questions; and interviewees have used them to reinforce or push back against my understanding, as well as to animate their own perceptions, expectations and experiences, and to propose, speculate or prefigure answers. For example, an important insight that was made visible to me during one such interview was that if public bodies were to generate new spaces where island-wide economic life is possible and probable, a key payoff might be spillover effects into wider economic life. In some instances, I have gifted an artefact with the interviewee to act as a grateful trace of our interaction. Lastly, I have used these artefacts to explain my research project to the wider sociolegal community in formal presentations; and as a constant private reminder—in my pocket, on a shelf—of the people and ideas at the heart of my research .

Surfacing challenges and solutions

One of the central issues that must be addressed as part of any effort to imagine, let alone reconstruct, island-wide economic life in Cyprus is the tangle of property rights that have been lost, gained, enhanced and eviscerated as a consequence of the mass displacement of persons. I explored this issue in a full-day experiment with Fiona Mullen--a Cyprus-based consultant with a long record of innovative policy analysis on island-wide economic life.

The session took place at the Home for Cooperation—a community centre located within the United Nations-controlled buffer zone that aims 'to act as a bridge-builder between separated communities, memories and visions' (Home for Cooperation website). I brought with me a selection of artefacts including modular LEGO components, found beach stones and a vinyl mat printed with an outline of the island but no place names or dividing lines (Figure 3.3). As anticipated, this map provided an important provocative space in which to speculate about possible island-wide futures. The LEGO components provided a relatively comfortable, effective and immediate means of expression.

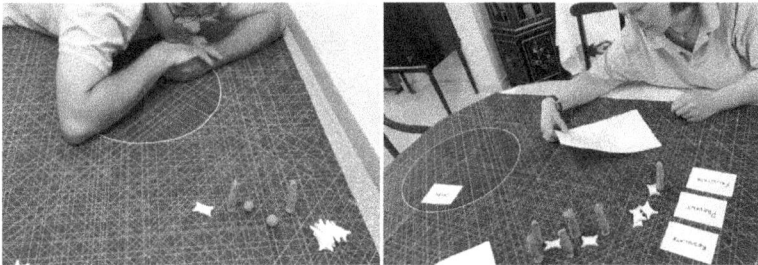

Figure 3.3 Economists Alexandros Apostolides and Fiona Mullen using a printed vinyl mat and clay figures to explore law and economic life in Cyprus. Images: Amanda Perry-Kessaris.

We focused on the question: What trade-offs will lie at the heart of any potential regime for addressing the impact of the division on Cyprus on property rights? Over the course of the experimental iterations, Fiona Mullen developed an increasingly precise visual, and then verbal, language for communicating about the actors and factors at the heart of this question. She used that language to work through with increasing precision a range of complex intersecting scenarios and specify a set of solutions. Eventually, she chose to summarize her findings in narrated pen and paper sketches (Figure 3.4).

The session offered many invaluable insights to me as a newcomer to the property rights issue. More importantly, Fiona Mullen identified to important benefits to her that arose from the session: A new category of property rights holder became visible to her; and she immediately began 'thinking of how to visually build up' an 'argument rather than just dump it on' those with whom she would be engaging in the coming days (Personal Communication, 21 December 2016).

Pop-up collections

We can gather together a range of materials or objects to make visible more complex networks of ideas. In so doing, we are building a collection not only within the 'conventional meaning' of 'formally curated set of "like"

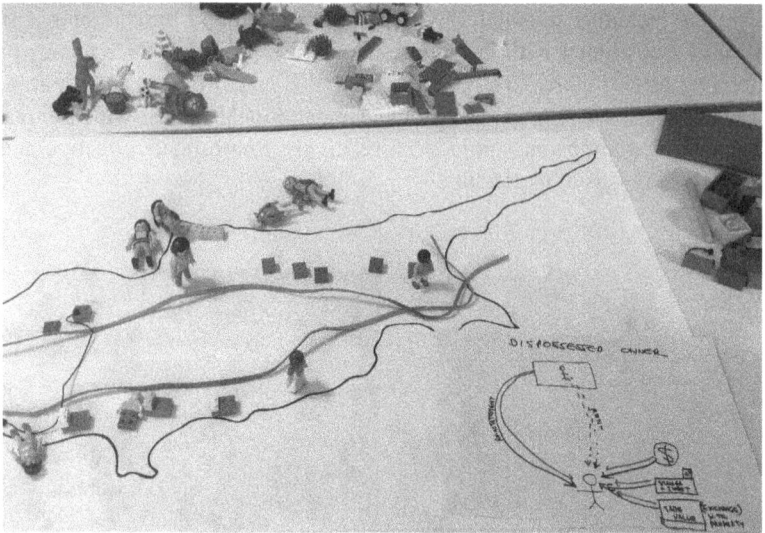

Figure 3.4 Models and sketches of possible solutions to conflicting claims to property as part of a negotiated settlement on the future of divided Cyprus made by economist Fiona Mullen, Home for Cooperation, December 2016. Image: Amanda Perry-Kessaris.

objects', but also in the more 'dynamic', 'diffuse' and 'fluid' sense of an 'assemblage'.[5] Looking at such gatherings through the lens of assemblage, we can see 'clusters' of things that are 'vibrant' and 'have agency' in space and over time, and 'as a whole', in relation to each other and within human relations (Woodward 2020, 77–81).

Any museum can be seen as part of an assemblage including, for example, their collectors, artefacts, exhibition notes, audiences, premises, collection catalogues and databases.[6] These can be rendered more generally or particularly dynamic and vibrant through internal or external re-framings. For example, in 'Displays of Power' (2019), the Grant Museum of Zoology reframed its collection through the lens of empire. Transparent film with fresh curatorial notes was applied to the existing display cases to locate animals, laws and humans—including interloping colonial scientists and collectors and those indigenous people who often made their work possible, but sometimes were destroyed by it—in 'a natural history of empire' (see Figure 5.7, Chapter 5).[7] Alternatively, assemblages can be made more dynamic and vibrant by an external reframing undertaken by someone outside of the formal museum ecosystem.[8] Such external assemblages might be thought of as part of the 'anti-collection'—that is, that section of the 'universe of publication' that is 'not held in the local collection' of the library or museum (Van der Veer Martens 2011, 568 Quoting Ross Atkinson)—and they might relate to one or many formal collections. Finally, an assemblage may be created in an exhibition that makes no reference to any formal collection but rather emerges entirely out of a research event.

Each of these assemblage strategies is explored among the following paragraphs that detail one project—the 'Pop-up museum of legal objects' project—and two standalone events, the 'Making sociolegal research visible and tangible' workshop and the 'IEL pop-up collection'. In each case, I acted as a (co)facilitator to 'encourage', 'close down', 'question' and 'increase or slow down the momentum', prompting participants to listen to each other narrating what they have made, to engage more deeply with each contribution by 'metaphorically double-clicking' on particular aspects of it such as 'such as its size or colour … or its relationship' to the whole, to 'gift' each other insights around what seems to be 'true' in or 'missing' from what they were making and to ask how all the participant's contributions 'might connect with each other and how they can be adjusted'. As is often the case, such post-making discussions were as productive as the making itself (James and Brookfield 2014, 116, 118 and 124–5).

Pop-up museum of legal objects

The 'Pop-up museum of legal objects' is an evolving online collection of commentaries produced by sociolegal researchers, each of which explores the relationship between an artefact and a particular research project or theme.[9] Twenty researchers to date have contributed to this particular collection by selecting a 'chosen object', usually from a curated collection, and following the process detailed in the 'Objects' brief in Chapter 5. By focusing first on the object as a material thing, then on its past and present social and cultural context, they have been able to both generate new ideas about their research and also to use the object to communicate those ideas to themselves and to others.

The collection originated in a series of in-person gatherings (see Perry-Kessaris 2017a). The first event was held in 2017 at the British Museum. It began in the Great Court where we collectively made flat printed event guides—in which I had placed images and brief descriptions of our chosen objects—into folded booklets. The majority of the day was spent touring the Museum together around each chosen object, listening to a commentary and receiving the gift of a 'trace' made for us by the presenter. Such traces included a strip of paper printed with the sound waves produced by speaking the words inscribed on an anti-slavery medallion and a Kilner jar of wild rice from Rice Lake in the traditionally Anishinaabe territory of south-eastern Ontario, Canada. We ended back in the Great Court where, in among the visiting school children and tourists, we made clay replicas of our chosen objects and exhibited them on a display mat designed specifically for this purpose (Figure 3.5).

After the event, we shared images of the 'traces' assembled in our respective homes and offices. Designers speak of 'tracing', or generating a 'trace' from, as distinct from documenting, an event or experience. Perceptions differ and evolve, and it takes time both for them to emerge and determine whether and how they might be 'interwoven' and made accessible to others (Akama 2018, 92 et seq. See also Pink 2011; Stickdorn 2018a, 75). To speak in terms of traces is to acknowledge that, on the one hand, it can be useful, often generative, to capture a sense of an event or experience, and/but, on the other hand, complete capture is impossible and often undesirable.

Reflecting on the process of presenting in the museum, participants remarked: 'What a unique opportunity! It invited me to place my object in context, in place, and to put it into conversation with other objects discussed in the workshop'. On making a trace: 'I spent a week on mine and it really changed the way I thought about the object and about my research'; and 'productive in unexpected ways, particularly in terms of the engagement with different (actually and potentially useful) materials. I had not thought of my legal research objects as being so readily interpretable in material form'. On making replicas on-site: 'FUN!!! Also very helpful for the process of identifying the core of my interest in the object that I chose for the workshop'. A chance 'to let all the information sink

Figure 3.5 Scenes from the legal objects workshop. British Museum, March 2017. Clockwise from top left: Rose Parfitt introduces the Battle Adwa; Ruth Buchanan and Jeffery Hewitt co-make a model of an Anishinabe ceremonial/British military drum; participants gather around a pop-up exhibition of their models in the Great Court; the author exploring the collection of gifted traces at home. Images: Amanda Perry-Kessaris.

in and process' and to see 'links and distinctions between such disparate objects'. 'Having seen common themes surface throughout the day, making and bringing together the models made tangible those connections and commonalities. A sort of material manifestation of the dialogue that we have taken part in'.

The second event was held in the same year during the SLSA annual conference in Newcastle and began, once again, with the collective making of event guide booklets. This time, participants placed pre-made models of their chosen objects onto a bespoke display mat at the beginning of the day. Once the presentations were complete, the exhibition was transferred to the main meeting room where a looped slide show projected text about the represented objects for the conference as a whole. One participant reflected:

> The opportunity to view the models together [exhibited in the main meeting room] led to a fruitful discussion with other delegates. We considered the ways in which incorporating images of models into our

research data might aid understanding and enable the creation of previously unarticulated constructions of the research process.

On the underpinning design of these events, one participant reflected that:

> Going through your list made me realise just how many contextual elements you've added to structure the production and presentation of our commentaries, which is such a contrast to a standard conference paper existing almost entirely in isolation. It's something I've found very helpful in doing the writing and presenting and it's also really engaged me in the project's rationale.

During each event, the objects and participants were assembled in live Twitter threads. Object-based commentaries from both events were assembled in an online exhibition, and some extended commentaries were published in a special issue of a journal. These collections, together with the material exhibitions held on location at each event and the researchers that generated them, can be seen as sociolegal research assemblages—assemblages that both reflect and sustain a sense of research community. As one participant reflected, seeing the commentaries online 'enabled a more objective consideration of the need for all researchers to be reflexive about power dynamics and to be mindful of their role in co-constructing the research environment'.

'Making sociolegal research visible and tangible' workshop

The 'Making sociolegal research visible and tangible' workshop was held in March 2018 at the Institute of Advanced Legal Studies and involved eight sociolegal researchers.[10] The day began with an informal communal analysis of answers to five questions that had been provided in advance by each participant, and then reformatted into a consistent collection and displayed on individual sheets of A4 paper in a grid format on a table. The questions were: What is your current research question? How are you going about answering it? Why is your project important for (a) theory and (b) practice? What problems are you having/do you anticipate? What do you think you might gain from making your research visible and tangible? As we discussed the answers, we moved the papers around, aligning and stacking them to reveal similarities and differences between the answers and the projects more generally.

Apart from a brief excursion to the British Museum to complete a tour of legal objects I had developed and detailed in a printed guide, the majority of the day was spent making: First, modular making, using

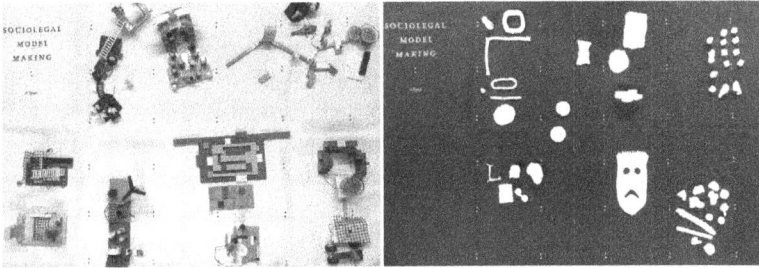

Figure 3.6 Exhibiting modular (left) and bespoke (right) model-making outputs as part of the 'Making sociolegal research visible and tangible' workshop co-organized with Diamond Ashiagbor, March 2018. Image: Amanda Perry-Kessaris.

LEGO to communicate core components of each project; then found making, using images of museum artefacts chosen by participants in advance to generate new insights into the projects; and finally, bespoke making, using clay to make representations of key concepts, actors or themes from the projects. At each stage, the resulting artefacts were exhibited together on one of two cloth mats produced as part of the Sociolegal Model-Making project, once again forming assemblages—in this case, temporary and material—that both reflect and sustain a sense of research community (Figure 3.6).

IEL pop-up collection

The IEL Collective is a collaboration of academics and practitioners from across the world directed at working inclusively to 'stimulate conversations about plurality, representation and criticality' in the field of international economic law. In the terminology of this volume, it is devoted to establishing meaningful research relations and calls for the proactive generation of shared spaces in which multiple conceptual frames, empirical examples and normative agendas can be explored. Sometimes the sacrifices—contortions, erasures and superficialities—required to make multiplicities cohere by holding them, even temporarily, in a shared, structured space, may prove excessive. But if we want to contribute meaningfully, we must try. Might an exhibition help? This was the question that motivated me to propose the co-production of a pop-up collection as part of the IEL Collective inaugural conference held at Warwick Law School in November 2019.

Delegates from across the world, many of whom had never met, were invited to bring with them to the conference an artefact (object or image) that they felt was relevant to their approach to, or understanding of, international economic law, which was either found or made and would fit on an A5 page. Some were bound to hesitate or baulk at engaging with such an unfamiliar activity, but the warm, inclusive and non-hierarchical approach of the Collective helped to mitigate that risk. During the conference, the artefacts were placed on designed A5 cards in the form of a grid. Arrows printed on the cards indicated possible points of contact or influence between the artefacts and the approaches to or understandings of IEL that delegates intended them to represent. Exhibitions—of objects, film, photos, text, installations—are increasingly curated by or for researchers from the natural and social sciences, not only as 'alternative forms of dissemination' but also as 'a way of asking research questions' (Woodward 2020, 169). The IEL pop-up collection served as a place for discussion and reflection throughout the event, and delegates were invited to engage physically with the artefacts. For example, Figure 3.7:

> shows delegates handling and discussing an artefact made by Gamze Erdem Turkelli to represent International Economic Law as a black box. On opening we find plain notes representing the international economic activities (trade, investment, aid) and elaborate bejewelled notes representing the promised benefits of engaging in such activities—for

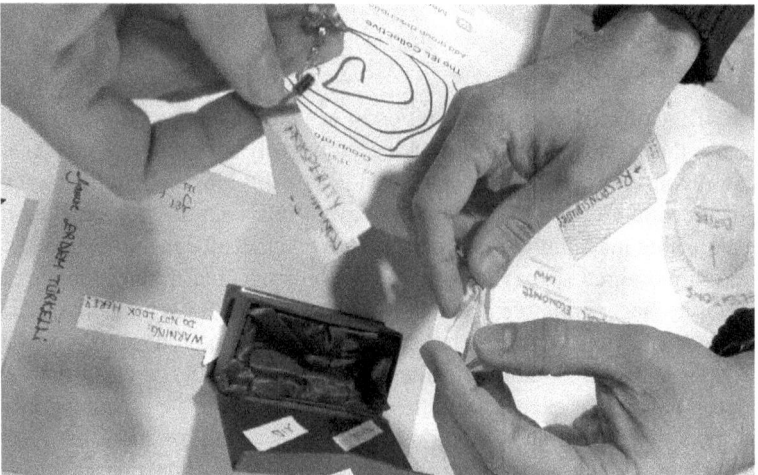

Figure 3.7 Interacting with bespoke artefacts exhibited during the inaugural conference of the IEL Collective, 6–7 November 2019, University of Warwick. Image: Amanda Perry-Kessaris

example, prosperity. Eventually, we realise that the box contains another hidden layer full of decentred concerns such as climate change, colonialism and gender.

(Perry-Kessaris 2020, 1442)

Each assemblage described previously—whether in a shared journey through a museum, in the space of a display mat or an online repository or social media output—opens the possibility for generating new insights into, and connections between, the researchers, objects and projects with which they were associated. Now stored on a shelf, in a drawer or on a desk in our homes or workspaces, the models and traces made along the way may continue to generate flashes of memory and insight.

Clarifying and influencing thinking and practice around hate crime

An opportunity to test how designerly ways might enhance the ability of sociolegal research to make meaningful contributions to the wider world arose through my methodological involvement in *Facing All the Facts*. This stakeholder-led project addressed challenges around the reporting and recording of hate crime across six European countries and was conducted on behalf of a diverse partnership of 11 public authorities and civil society organizations from nine countries (Perry 2019). The project had three inter-connected objectives: To develop a holistic, evidence-based understanding of the nature and effectiveness of the 'systems' for reporting and recording of hate crime in the project countries; to generate reflective spaces in which the actors within those 'systems' could share perceptions, expectations and experiences and identify solutions; and to shift those actors and systems towards more victim-centred, system-based and action-oriented mindsets and practices. The project methodology supported those objectives through a combination of 'traditional', participatory and designerly research methods (Perry-Kessaris and Perry 2020). Here I will focus on how designerly ways were deployed to mitigate the risks and enhance the rewards associated with participatory strategies.

Stakeholders from a wide range of public and civil society sectors were brought together in a series of hands-on participatory workshops loosely akin to design sprints. Participants had Often participants had never met and had reason to be wary of each other because they were deliberately selected for their diversity of perspectives—for example, they generally included 'activists with direct experience of supporting victims, police and prosecutors with direct experience of investigating/prosecuting and recording hate crimes, statisticians responsible for reviewing data and deciding on publication, and ministry officials responsible for resource allocation'

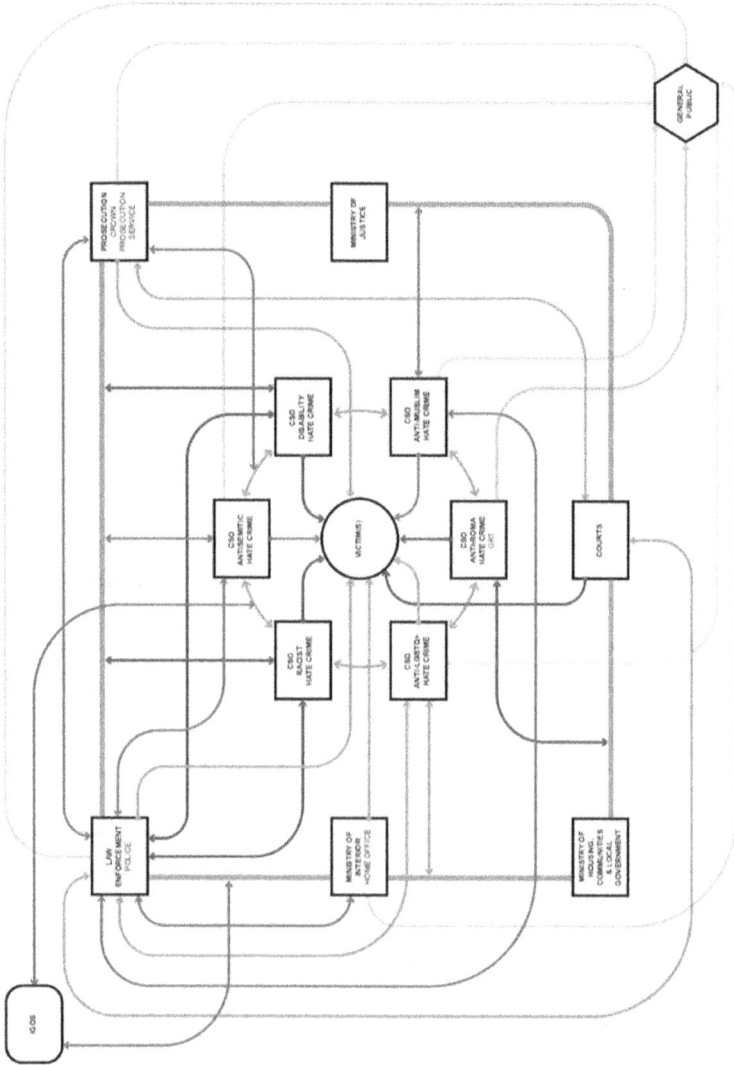

Figure 3.8 Detail from England and Wales System map, 17 Perry (2019) Connecting on Hate Crime Data in England and Wales. Brussels, CEJI. Image licence under CC 4.0.

(Perry-Kessaris and Perry 2020). A sense of structured freedom is essential in order for participation to be possible and productive in such circumstances: 'The boundaries of the communicative space, the type of participation leadership, opportunities to express anxiety and the balance between order and chaos must be continually negotiated'; and researchers and participants must able to accommodate results that are 'necessarily paradoxical and contradictory' (Bergold and Thomas 2012, 14).

During the workshops, participants completed activities designed to enable them to engage with each other as 'expert critical friends, to see and experience things from each other's point of view', to pool information and best practice and to consider how they might support each other in the future. As part of each consensus-building activity, groups of diverse actors worked iteratively to plot facts and expert perceptions about how hate crime is reported and recorded in their jurisdiction onto a large adhesive wall-mounted surface—'attach[ing], mov[ing] and remov[ing] labelled cards and coloured string in a physical process of negotiation and debate across professional, social and cultural "divides"'. Following moderated discussion, participants were asked to agree priority actions for improvement. The result was a prototype of the actual/potential national 'system'. These prototypes then informed a set of formal graphic artefacts and a set of text-based national reports (Figure 3.8). The maps functioned as boundary objects—shared spaces in which to identify and discuss disparate perceptions, expectations and experiences and about how things are and how they might be—not only during the workshops but also over the course of the project and in the final reports. In this way, making things visible and tangible promoted a more communal and collaborative orientation throughout, and in the ensuing months, participants reported that their interpersonal relations and plans for the future changed as a result (Perry-Kessaris and Perry 2020).

Notes

1 Sophie Woodward uses the term 'material ethnography' to capture activities that use materiality to understand the world, and/or seek to understand the material world itself, and are 'holistic', 'immersive', 'open-ended', embrace 'serendipity' and use 'multiple methods' including participation, observation, interviews and conversations (Woodward 2020, 118–22).

2 The artefacts are stored in an online repository—A Site, available at amandaperrykessaris.org. The primary artefact, designed to downloaded and printed lo-fi on A4 paper, is A Guide, in which three accessible modes of model-making are explained. Secondary artefacts made available for download are A Proposition, in which a call is made to sociolegal researchers to engage in model-making; A Space, which is a luxury artefact on which to place sociolegal models, designed

to be downloaded and printed at large scale on canvas, and two longer publications designed to be viewed on-screen or printed on A4; A Context, in which the theory and practice informing the project are introduced; and A Portfolio, in which the project design process is visualized.

3 I have also used LEGO to communicate to myself when developing the structure of an article (Perry-Kessaris 2017b).

4 All such documentation is available via amandaperrykessaris.org.

5 'Assemblage' was proposed as a unit of analysis by Giles Deleuze and Félix Gauttari, was substantially developed as conceptual lens through which to understand all social relations by Manuel DeLanda, and has since been adopted as a material method within archaeology: Woodward 2020, 77–81.

6 Some, such as Bruno Latour, Michel Callon and other proponents of actor–network theory (ANT) argue that 'people and things' are 'produced by' and 'exist in relations' with each other, and that '[a]gency emerges from these networks' (Woodward 2020, 20–1). But Ingold argues that the ideas question of agency only arises if we reduce 'things to objects' with 'arbitrary starting points' (an image in the designer's eye) and 'an equally arbitrary end point (the allegedly finished work)', thereby ignoring the 'vitality' of 'its materials' which ensure that it will never be 'truly "finished"' (except in the eyes of curators and purchasers who require it to be so)' (Ingold 2013, 103–5).

7 See also the 2010 telling by former director of the British Museum Neil Macgregor of 'a history of the world in 100 objects'. His account centres on objects, but their relations with each other and their roles in human relations are emphasized throughout.

8 See also 'Thinking into | about practice', a collection of commentaries by academics and practitioners each exploring the relevance of a given image or object to the field of law and development, available under 'collections' at amandaperrykessaris.org.

9 This project was organized in collaboration with Lisa Dickson and Sophie Vigneron. The commentaries formed the basis of an online collection available under 'collections' at amandaperrykessaris.com; as well as 15 articles in a 2017 special issue of the *Northern Ireland Legal Quarterly*.

10 This event was co-organized with Diamond Ashiagbor and funded by the Kent Law School and the Institute of Advanced Legal Studies.

4 Reconstructing pasts, speculating futures

The preceding chapters have explored designerly ways (Chapters 1 and 2) and illustrated how some of those ways might be adapted by sociolegal researchers acting as non-expert designers (Chapter 3). This chapter explores what might become possible if sociolegal researchers were to collaborate with expert designers. It draws attention to how experts from architecture, speculative design and performance arts have directed their specialized technical skillsets towards substantive fields of inquiry that are of direct sociolegal concern, focusing in particular on how they prompt and facilitate themselves, and those whom they seek to influence, or with whom they seek to collaborate, to be imaginative about pasts, presents and futures, as well as the relationships between them.

Imagination is about moving 'sideways and beyond', 'away from the well-trodden', in order 'to sniff out the subtle indicators of possibility' and to see 'different aspects of a situation or individual and their potential'. Our 'capacity to imagine is part of what makes us human' and it is essential to any effort to 'conceive of, and realize' something new (James and Brookfield 2014, 3 and 57–8), and is vital to anyone who wishes to work with the idea of law. We legal, including sociolegal, types regularly create imaginaries—some dark and dystopian, others bright and optimistic; some retrospective, some prospective.[1] We must imagine, not only because law is fundamentally imaginary, but also because nothing in the pluriverse of social and legal 'arrangements' is 'natural, necessary, or sacrosanct' (Unger 2021, 4). So another way is always possible. But it is difficult to, on the one hand, 'do justice to' the existing 'richness and complexity' of the world as it currently exists while simultaneously, on the other hand, 'opening up to radical, speculative inquiry into the potentials of human life' (Ingold 2013, 6). It is perhaps especially difficult for sociolegal researchers operating, as many of us do, within the confines of deductive thinking, and so failing, as we sometimes do, to pay adequate methodological attention to the wider conceptual, empirical, normative, analytical, processual and relational

DOI: 10.4324/9780367177683-4

shifts that imaginative work necessarily entails. That is the special expertise of designers, who tend to understand that negotiating the actual-potential requires thinking and action that is simultaneously practical (concrete, coherent, doable), critical (exposing and questioning empirical realities, as well as conceptual and normative frames) and imaginative (speculative, generative, future-focused), and whose mindsets, processes and strategies make it all more possible and probable.

What is distinctive about designers is not only that they embrace imagination more explicitly and proactively than most sociolegal researchers, but also that they use their creative skills to make imaginaries visible and tangible. In so doing, they create structured-yet-free, potentially enabling ecosystems in which we can explore what is, what was, and what ought or ought not to be or have been. Here 'creativity' does not imply a 'lack of control', or 'the visitation of the muse, the genesis of genius, or the quick-fix solution that just springs up in your mind unbidden'. It may be associated with 'serendipity ... unexpected connection, chance meetings, and seeing the everyday and familiar in new ways'; but it does not imply 'a permanent move into fantasy' (James and Brookfield 2014, 54, 57–8 and 60). And it requires specialist techniques.[2]

The following sections draw first on the practice of forensic architecture to demonstrate how designerly ways can prompt and facilitate the reconstruction of pasts, followed by the practices of artists Sarah Browne, Jesse Jones and Jack Tan to illustrate how designerly ways can prompt and facilitate 'what if' speculation about, and even the 'as if' prefiguration of, alternative futures.

(Re)construction

Forensic architecture is a field of practice in which architectural mindsets, strategies and processes are applied for investigative purposes, typically in order to assign legal liability to an architect in the course of an insurance claim.[3] In the hands of Forensic Architecture—a research agency based at Goldsmiths, University of London—the power of expert architectural mindsets, strategies and processes is instead turned back on states and corporations.

Architecture, like design more broadly, 'operates' across three 'sites': The 'field' which, in Forensic Architecture investigations, is where 'violence takes place and where traces are left'; the laboratory or 'studio' is where 'material is processed and composed into evidence'; and the forum is 'where it is presented'. As part of their wider mission to 'salvage' forensics from the 'grip of state agencies', they aim first, to open up these sites and, second, to 'erode the differences between' them so that each can enrich and challenge the other. A consistent theme running through their 'counterforensic' practice is to expose that which is 'close to and under the threshold of detectability'—a threshold often set by states and corporations.[4] So they regularly draw on data, such as mobile phone footage and witness testimonies, that have been spontaneously captured by survivors or otherwise affected persons as events unfold (Weizman 2017, 28–30, 65–6). For example, PATTRN is a platform to which diffuse activists, researchers and monitors can upload individual pieces of multimedia information—in one case, mobile phone footage of suspected Russian tanks in eastern Ukraine—so that they can be gathered and visualized in relation to each other, thereby revealing 'patterns and trends' of legal significance.[5] Sometimes they engage survivors and others in systematic, intentional data gathering after the event. For example, Yazidi community members were trained to use simple, lo-fi methods and materials—cameras attached to kites using plastic bottles and rubber bands—to document the destruction of their cultural heritage in a format compatible with hi-fi digital modelling techniques (Forensic Architecture website).

Adopting something akin to 'the imaginary gaze of a future archaeologist looking back to the present', Forensic Architecture gather 'structures, infrastructures, objects, environments, actors and incidents' into 'evidence assemblages'. They may, for example, juxtapose images of 'before' and 'after' of official versus unofficial images and regulated building plans and unregulated buildings, or collect and categorize images to reveal patterns of behaviour or outcome. A more specifically architectural, and more technically complex, strategy is to use software such as Blender to create three-dimensional digital, navigable, 'architectural image complexes'. The process begins with a precise digital model of the relevant space. Visual data such as photographic and video material—fragments which, taken individually, and with a non-expert eye, are little more than morbid mementos—are then mapped across the spatial frame of the model and into the temporal frame of an event timeline (Weizman 2017, 58 and 98).

Theirs is an 'engaged civil practice that seeks to articulate public claims' within and beyond, the 'technical, neutral domain of expert specialists' and the 'well-established court system and its protocols'. For example, they are conscious that visible and/or tangible artefacts 'are usually intuitively understood by both the legal professional and the general public' (Weizman, 59). So they disseminate their evidence to the legal forum and the public forum in digital and physical models, some of which we can think of as more evidentiary—for example, building surveys, models and annotated maps, and some of which we can think of as more testimonial—for example, narrated animations and videos. These expertly designed artefacts communicate complex information in ways that are generative and provocative, but also systematic and precise. All forensic science is 'an *aesthetic* practice' in that it 'depends on both the modes and the means by which incidents are sensed, recorded, and presented'. It 'seeks to slow down time'; to 'intensif[y] sensibility to space, matter and image'; and 'to devise new modes' for narrating claims as to what is true. Courts are well-used to forensic evidence, but they are uncomfortable with its aesthetic dimensions that tend in legal minds to be associated with 'manipulation, emotional or illusionary trickery', 'a lack of seriousness' and bias. So those wishing to contribute forensically to a legal domain face a 'paradox'—on the one hand, they must draw on 'aesthetics and imagination' to unearth, assess and present facts, but on the other hand, they must somehow maintain the idea of 'truth as ... already simply there'. For Forensic Architecture, the balance is clear: They are not engaged in conventional 'positivistic' forensic science. Rather, they practice 'the art of making claims using matter and media, code and calculation, narrative and performance' (Weizman 2017, 75, 83 and 94). They are making and communicating a sense of things by 'develop[ing], disseminat[ing], and employ[ing] new techniques for evidence gathering and presentation', and they are doing so specifically 'in the service of human rights and environmental investigations, and in support of communities exposed to state violence and persecution' (Forensic Architecture website). From 'microphysical details' in the material world, they 'pull' not only reconstructions of what happened but also 'longer threads' that can be used to 'reconnect' what happened to a wider social and political context. So it is that the artefacts that Forensic Architecture produce, and their associated claims, are often much broader, deeper and more critical than courts and public inquiries are willing or able to accommodate (Weizman 2017, 9, 11, 51, 64 and 65).

The following sections explore how Forensic Architecture's digital models have been used to 'rebuild', 'explore' and communicate about responsibilities, experiences and narratives, and how in offering the chance to reconstruct pasts, Forensic Architecture's practices also open spaces for alternative possible futures for individuals and communities. Information in these sections is primarily drawn from text and video documenting three Forensic Architecture investigations: A factory fire, a drone strike and a police killing. We might think of each of these investigations as a 'performative process of working through trauma that is stuck between the time of too-early and too-late' (Enright and Kinsella 2021, 18). While in the case of the Ali Enterprises factory fire that process is performed primarily by the researcher; in the case of the Mir Ali drone strike and the killing of Harith Augustus, some of the working through is performed directly by the survivors of the trauma. In this 'working through', the 'residual traumatic effects ... are no longer a past catastrophe, but rather a series of affective events that bear upon'—but are not necessarily 'reproduce[d] in'—the present

(Enright and Kinsella 2021, 19). And it is perhaps in achieving this difficult balance between productively activating, yet not destructively reproducing, trauma that practices such as Forensic Architecture most profoundly distinguish themselves.

...*of responsibility*

On 11 September 2012, 259 people died in a fire at the Ali Enterprises textile factory in Karachi. Forensic Architecture was commissioned by the European Centre for Constitutional and Human Rights—an independent, non-profit legal and educational organization—to investigate. While the national authorities focused their attention on who may have started the fire, Forensic Architecture started from the normative assumption that fires can and do happen in factories, and building design ought—morally, legally and according to core design principles—to mitigate their impact. Furthermore, they started from the empirical knowledge that the building can 'sense' our physical, social and political behaviour. Any 'material object can', with the necessary expertise, 'be read as a sensor. But buildings might be among the best sensors of societal and political change' because they 'are anchored in space' (Weizman 2017, 28–30 and 54). As such they offer a stable point of reference in an otherwise open, complex, networked and dynamic context.

They assembled satellite and ground-level photography and video footage, witness sketches and testimonies, as well as previous investigative reports by Pakistani authorities to create a 3D digital model of the factory building and to reconstruct its everyday use. All of this information was placed on a timeline to map the spread of the fire. Onto this assemblage, they pinned specific provisions of national legislation, such as the Factories Act 1934, as well as the SA8000 Social Accountability guidelines under which the factory was certified (see Social Accountability International. Undated). Using computational fluid dynamics to model alternative smoke pathways, and crowd simulation to model alternative flows of people, they revealed that safe evacuation of all employees would have been possible had regulations been followed. In short, 'design and management decisions failed to prevent injury and casualties' and even 'augmented the death toll' (Forensic Architecture website). We can think of this model, as well as the process of building it, as generating a structured-yet-free space within which to explore different propositions about possible relationships between, on the one hand, the decisions of commercial and regulatory actors and, on the other hand, the lives of workers .

The results of the investigation were submitted to the Regional Court in Dortmund, Germany, where survivors and victims' family members have filed a civil case against a German clothing retailer that was supplied by

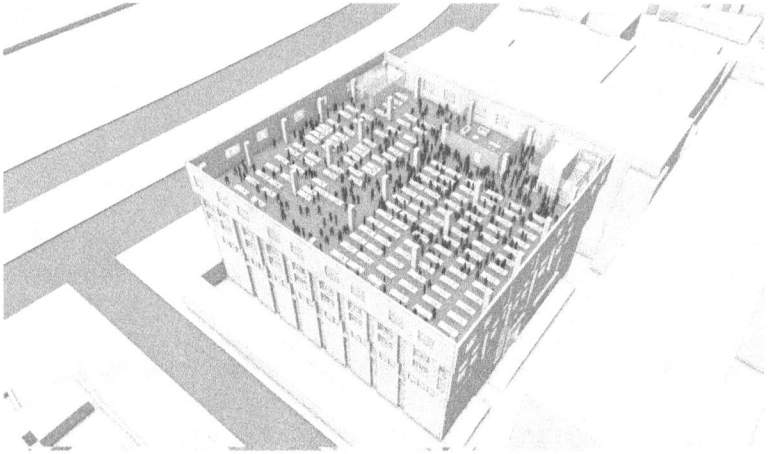

Figure 4.1 Still from Forensic Architecture (2018) 'The Ali Enterprises Factory Fire'. An aerial view of the top floor of the factory identifies overcrowding as a cause of the substantial loss of life during the fire. Image: Forensic Architecture, 2018.

the factory. A video version is available on the Investigations section of the Forensic Architecture website (Figure 4.1).[6] We can think of this video as enabling each contributor, and then every viewer, to activate their imagination to practical and critical ends.

...of experience

Forensic Architecture have developed a strategy known as 'situated testimony' in which a witness is filmed as they reconstruct the scene of an event using 3D digital modelling, 'exploring and accessing their memories of the episode in a controlled and secure manner', in collaboration with an architectural researcher. Here architecture is functioning as a mnemonic technique in the tradition of Cicero and Quintilian who famously advised that when planning a speech, we ought to associate each element with a particular object in a particular room, and then when delivering it we ought to imagine ourselves walking from object to object, room to room (Weizman 2017, 65).

On 4 October 2010, five people were killed when a US drone struck a home in Mir Ali, near the border between Afghanistan and Pakistan. An investigation into the strike was commissioned by the UN Special

Figure 4.2 Still from Forensic Architecture (2013) 'Drone Strike in Mir Ali'. Digital reconstruction of a US drone strike that hit a home in Mir Ali, North Waziristan, Pakistan, killing five people. One of the surviving witnesses, pictured, worked with Forensic Architecture in Dusseldorf to build a digital model of her former home. Image: Forensic Architecture, 2013.

Rapporteur on Counter-Terrorism and Human Rights. The investigation was conducted through meetings held in Dusseldorf between a model maker, a witness and her lawyer. So the team had 'no access to the site, no ruins to study, and no photographs except a satellite image that showed nothing except the blurred contours of her house'. Instead, the iterative, experimental process of architectural model-making generated a structured-yet-free space in which she could 'access' and 'perform' the memories of her life in the house with those who were killed, and of the destruction of all of that (Forensic Architecture website). In the video documenting the investigation, we see her piecing together place, people and events—at one point calling out 'Stop. Now I remember' (Figure 4.2). The witness's primary aim was to raise awareness of what it is like to live with the constant threat of drones. But in the process, she also retrieved details that had previously been obscured by trauma (Weizman 2017, 46–7). The results of the investigation were included in a Report of the UN Special Rapporteur for Counter-Terrorism to the UN General Assembly and were disseminated to the public on the Forensic Architecture website and in multiple exhibitions (Forensic Architecture website).

In another investigation centring on situated testimony, survivors of a Syrian torture prison were able to collaborate with architectural researchers to construct 3D digital models of a building of which they had barely been able to catch sight due to blindfolds and isolation. Instead, the reconstruction drew on their perceptions 'of differences in temperature, moisture, light, vibrations and echoes'. The resulting digital models 'induce[d] further recollections'. Some of these were edited into short videos and treated as 'memory objects' to be 'placed' in an interactive digital model of the prison building that would serve as an architecturally grounded 'archive' (Weizman 2017, 91). Now that they were made visible, their memories could be owned and honoured.

We can think of situated testimony as prompting and facilitating each witness to activate their imagination, and thereby, the imagination of every other viewer, to practical and critical ends .

…of narratives

The Superintendent of the Chicago Police Department characterized the shooting to death of Harith Augustus on 14 July 2018 as 'a split-second decision'. As the Forensic Architecture video investigation of this killing observes, the 'concept of a "split second" is often invoked as a legal defence when the police are investigated for use of lethal force' and is 'treated as a black box that tends to isolate the incident from its context'. Forensic Architecture collaborated with a local journalism company, Invisible Institute, to draw attention to this habitual framing and to its consequences. Together, they reconstructed events surrounding the death of Harith Augustus in six video investigations, each on a scale of milliseconds, seconds, minutes, hours, days or years (Forensic Architecture website).

The videos on scales between milliseconds and hours explored, each with a different objective, a core data set: Audio and video from CCTV, police body cameras, dashboard cameras and an observational camera, as well as witness testimonies and police records. As in the Ali Enterprises factory fire investigation, that data was pinned to precise points in time and space, as well as to specific provisions in legislation and guidance. For example, the 'minutes' video opens with the observations that 'No evidence ever speaks for itself, certainly not a silent video'. It then uses witness statements and police testimony to add back in sound that was lost because of the failure by police, in breach of departmental guidance, to switch their body cameras to 'event mode'. By contrast, the 'millisecond' video combines the core data set with expert input from a neuroscientist around instinctive decision and response times in order to highlight the failure of one officer to follow departmental guidance 'to create time' for de-escalation, and to attribute that failing to '"perceptual distortions" and racial bias' (Forensic Architecture website).

Figure 4.3 Still from Forensic Architecture (2019) 'The Killing of Harith Augustus: Hours'. Forensic Architecture conducted 'situated testimony' with the Invisible Institute's Trina Reynolds-Tyler to understand more about the protests that followed the killing of Harith Augustus. Image: Forensic Architecture, 2019.

As the scale expands to hours, days and years, so the scope of the videos expands to include the perceptions and experiences of local community members who protested in the immediate aftermath; those who campaigned over the ensuing days for the release of all official paper, audio and video files surrounding the killing; and those who place this killing among many other instances of violence in the preceding 100 years.

For their exhibition at the Chicago Biennial 2019, the team decided to focus on the expanded frame of hours, days and year, and did not include visual investigations relating to the milliseconds, seconds and minutes surrounding Harith Augustus' death. They wanted 'to open a space for critically important discussions about police violence and the politics of representation'. As the exhibition notes explain:

We are clear that our role is to conduct a counter-investigation to contest the official narrative; and we are equally clear about our responsibility to make the results of our investigation universally available and to share the techniques we used to arrive at our conclusions. However, over the course of the project, we were confronted by an apparent contradiction between the necessity of looking and the difficulty of showing. We became increasingly concerned about presenting graphic scenes of police violence against a black man in the context of an exhibition, about the danger of foreclosing other ways of engaging with the life of Harith Augustus by repeatedly showing his last moments, and about inflicting difficult images on visitors who had not consented to view them.

With the full support of Harith Augustus's family, they have made the entire visual investigation available online and exhibited it elsewhere. It is in the knowledge of that support, tempered by the concerns raised by the investigative team in those exhibition notes, that I have selected the image from those investigations that appears here (Figure 4.3).

We can think of these videos as prompting and facilitating all those who contributed to them, and then every viewer, to be practical-critical-imaginative about pasts and about futures.

Speculation

This section explores the subfield of speculative design, which is devoted to conjuring and exploring future imaginaries. As preceding chapters have emphasized, design is a form of making—a 'search for something that is unknown in advance' (Juhani Palasmaa quoted in Ingold, 71). As such, it is in many ways future-focused. It requires 'anticipation'—that is, 'being one step ahead', 'look[ing] where you are going' and 'opening up a path and improvising a passage'; as opposed to 'preconception'—that is, 'thinking before seeing' or 'predetermining the final forms of things and all the steps needed to get there' (Ingold 2013, 69. See also Akama et al. 2018, 10–1). However, the future is not entirely 'empty'. It is, to some degree, pre-'loaded with our fantasies, aspirations and fears', and, to some extent, pre-formed by, or dependent upon, already-designed 'things, lifestyles and imaginaries'. So 'we can know something about what the future holds by studying the past and the present'. But at the same time, we can use the future—futurity, future-making, future-focus—to 'ask: *How can things be different?*' (Mazé 2016, 37–8. Emphasis original). Thinking about futures can afford us a critical distance from which to 'examine and compare with the here and now'. It can also generate a sense of agency—for example, in the sense that future 'we' may not be subject to our present-day constraints (Mazé 2016, 48–9).

Speculative designers join with futurology, speculative literature, drama and fine art and radical social science to argue that it is in speculating—and thereby 'loosen[ing], even just a bit', the 'grip' exerted by what we think of as 'reality' upon 'our imagination'—that we become truly 'critical'. Here the future is 'not a destination', nor 'something to be strived for'—it is not to be 'predict[ed] nor 'forecast'. Rather, 'possible futures' are seen as 'a medium to aid imaginative thought', as 'tools to better understand the present and to discuss the kind of future people want … and do not want' (Dunne and Raby 2013, 3. See also Akama et al. 2018, 10–1). Speculative interventions usually centre on a scenario that begins with the question 'what if'? Since the aim is not to teach or to moralize, but rather 'to open up spaces of debate and discussion', the scenarios are necessarily 'provocative, intentionally simplified and fictional'. They require that we 'suspend [our] disbelief and momentarily forget how things are now' (Dunne and Raby 2013, 3). They are intended to prompt and facilitate imaginings about how things might, for better or worse, be; and in so doing to provoke new experiences and relationships, and the emergence of new information about those experiences and relationships—to act as a 'catalyst for collectively redefining our relationship to reality' (Dunne and Raby 2013, 2–3). They are designed more to prompt and facilitate an 'opening up' and 'slow[ing] down', rather than to 'generate systematic data' or 'to capture things "as they are"'. Indeed, these methods may well produce 'fragmentary', even 'troubling', data that 'will not necessarily "make sense"' (Woodward 2020, 55–7 and 65–6).

What distinguishes speculative designers from others who work with futures is that they make the abstract dimensions of alternative futures visible and tangible. For example, they may build stage sets and props, or distribute 'cultural probes' (Gaver et al. 1999), which may or may not be fully functioning prototypes. These artefacts and spaces act either as 'synecdoches'—parts that represent the whole of the 'fictional world'—aimed at prompting and facilitating us to 'imagine the kind of society that would produce them, its values, beliefs and ideologies'; or as 'thought experiments-constructions'—in the form of reductio ad absurdum, counter-factuals or what-ifs--'through which to think about difficult issues' (Dunne and Raby 2013, 70, 76 and 80–8). These visible and/or tangible design speculations can afford a sense of structured freedom. And here freedom is structured less by an emphasis on 'predictive, prescriptive steps' (Akama et al. 2018, 10–1) in experimental processes and more by a communal attention to visible and tangible spaces and things. Freedom can be experienced not only in individual opportunities to imagine but also in shared opportunities for participants to imagine, for example, how they might relate differently to each other. On the one hand, these artefacts can give us 'permission to let [our] imaginations flow freely', on the other hand, they 'ground' those 'imaginings in everyday situations', and 'give material expression' to any 'insights generated' along the way (Dunne and Raby 2013, 6). In so doing, such material speculations can enable collaborative thinking and contribute to more meaningful relations. For example, in 2021, designer Stuart Candy brought an uncommon energy and depth to the proceedings of the United Nations Development Programme annual Innovation in Development event by interviewing each panellist on the theme of futures and development, then designing for them an artefact 'from the future' to arrive at their home a week before the event, to be referenced during the event discussion. In each case, the artefacts were intended to 'picture a far-reaching shift in relationships and power, manifested institutionally, affecting whatever we mean when we say "development"' (Candy 2021).

Speculative designers tend to set themselves the practical constraint of working within futures that are not only possible, but also actually probable and/or plausible, and refusing to dabble in things that are scientifically impossible (Dunne and Raby 2013, 5 and 12). They envisage their speculations 'facilitat[ing]', but not 'determin[ing]', the generation of millions of 'little utopias emerging from the bottom up', which, in turn, contribute to broader, systemic processes in which 'viable' options for social change are identified and made more possible and probable; and those 'factors that may lead to undesirable futures' can be reduced or mitigated (Dunne and Raby 2013, 6, 161 and 164). But because speculative interventions tend to aim for moral neutrality, not to 'suggest what *should* be' (Dunne and Raby 2013, 3), and because they tend to privilege the spectacular over the practical, speculative design remains an overwhelmingly conceptual enterprise: The idea is more important than the practical execution or effect. Of particular interest to the, generally more pragmatic, world of sociolegal researchers are calls from within for speculative designers to direct their skills beyond asking 'what if', and to work in support of normative and practical attempts to prefiguratively behave 'as if' (DiSalvo 2016; Asad 2019a and 2019b).

To act prefiguratively is to 'perform present-day life in the terms that are wished-for', both in order 'to experience' a 'better' present, and in order 'to advance' future 'change' (Cooper 2017, 335. See further in Maeckelbergh 2011; Davies 2017). Research from politics and, more recently, law tells us that prefigurative thinking and action opens up critical, optimistic spaces in which actual presents can be improved and potential futures can become more probable. Of particular relevance here is the work of Davina Cooper, of which I will highlight two strands. First, in work exploring alternative ways of thinking about states, Cooper (2017) has posed 'conceptual prefiguration' as a strategy by which everyday concepts 'such as property, markets and states' are 'approache[d] ... as if their meaning was otherwise and, more specifically, as if their meaning was one desired'. Second, in a project exploring the Future of Legal Gender (FLaG), Cooper has posed the strategy of 'prefigurative law reform' in which radical proposals are treated by researchers as if they were 'on the law reform table' (2020, 905). Both of these legal prefiguration strategies can prompt and facilitate re-framings of issues around which debate has become stuck. However, there is a risk that, to the extent that they are successful in creating places of 'refuge' and are 'insulated' from the entrenchments of the scholarly and wider world, such prefigurative strategies may remain too far removed from the fray to be trusted or to have a meaningful effect (Cooper 2020, 905). How might speculative design practices help to maximize the rewards and mitigate the risks of sociolegal prefiguration?

Designers already 'materially contribute to prefigurative politics' by creating artefacts for use in the course of the prefigurative actions of radical political activists. One example is the provision of 'crisis signage' to facilitate wayfinding during the Occupy campaigns. Carl DiSalvo (2016) argues that speculative design research methods are in some respects themselves prefigurative and could be used more actively to prompt and facilitate prefigurative action by making 'political speculations easier to experience, to experiment with, and ultimately to enact' (Di Salvo 2016, 34). Furthermore, Mariam Asad and her co-authors have proposed the term 'prefigurative design' to capture and promote design work that is done 'explicitly' for particular 'political or civic goals', and which 'articulat[es] those goals as design objects' and 'structure[s] design processes to actualize them' (Asad 2019a, 200:1 and 200:9. See further in 2019b). All research involves a degree of prefiguration—acting as if we are going somewhere, not only in order to have and to inspire confidence but to make any movement at all. Here the argument is that we might use specialist speculative design processes, especially iterative scenarios, and speculative design strategies, especially staging and prototypes, to experiment with different modes of sociolegal life and research design.

This volume includes a number of examples in which the non-expert use of designerly ways has aided more speculative, and then prefigurative, thinking and action. For example, Chapter 3 introduced the Facing All the Facts project whose participants, by collaborating in workshops and contributing to the production of formal artefacts, can be thought of as acting 'as if' systems for hate crime reporting and recording already existed; and the Island-Wide Economic Life project in which clay models and vinyl mats were used to conceptualize the roles of law in economic life in Cyprus. And Chapter 5 includes a brief that invites you to walk a labyrinth as if you were progressing through your research process. 'The following sections offer two examples of expert speculations that shed light on how, by collaborating with expert designers, sociolegal researchers and their users might be prompted and facilitated to speculate, and even to work prefiguratively.' Both examples are drawn from practitioners who self-describe as artists. Research methods from the creative arts, including performance arts such drama and dance, tend to be relatively 'evocative and provocative'; to emphasize 'people engaging with things processually' being 'open' to 'the unexpected'; and to draw on 'non-verbal, sensory, kinesthetic, material and imaginary ways of knowing'.[7] All of this can make them especially useful in thinking imaginatively across, or deeply within, languages and cultures (Woodward 2020, 68–9), and to inclusive, active and reflexive participation. As the following examples indicate, such creative methods can be made more accessible to sociolegal researchers—unsettling rather than alienating—when mediated through the structured-yet-free, practical-critical-imaginative ecosystems generated by designerly ways.

The Touching Contract

In the Shadow of the State (2016) is a project by artists Sarah Browne and Jesse Jones 'exploring statehood from the perspective of the female body'.[8] It emerged out of extensive collaboration with experts in the fields of medicine, law and material culture as well as music (*In the Shadow of the State* website). Here I will highlight one component of that project entitled *The Touching Contract*—a series of participatory events culminating in live participatory performances in Dublin and London, which 'work[ed] the emerging tension between the promise of official legal discourse and women's marginalised experiences of maternal, obstetric, and reproductive violence'. In their analysis of how artworks 'might play a role in the political, legal and aesthetical "working-through" of historical trauma', Máiréad Enright and Tina Kinsella describe *The Touching Contract* as 'deploy[ing] artistic and aesthetic devices' to generate a 'containing structure' or 'semi-structured "situation"' that is characterized by 'an atmosphere of vulnerable exposure to law and its related traumas', and in which 'the potential traumatic affects of historical injustice' are put '"in-play" for those participating in the performance to respond to, or not' (Enright and Kinsell 2021, 2 and 5). Structured-yet-free.

The performances themselves consisted of 'five rough phases' of a 'loosely choreographed, but improvised, pattern of movements' made by performers, both individually and with or to participants. Although the movements of the performers were 'deliberately open', and their significance was not explained, they nevertheless 'encouraged the participants to consider law's relationship to bodily oppression and control' in part because they were performed within a wider, culturally rich, visible and material structure (see Enright and Kinsella 2021, 6–7 and 12). They were not recorded in any way, what transpired being the business only of those who were present. However, photographs and a reflective/documentary film of the rehearsal, including staged interviews, give a sense of the techniques

Figure 4.4 Scenes from rehearsal for a performance of *The Touching Contract* in London with performers Rahel Vonmoos and Bernadette Iglich (above) and Odilia Egyiawan (below). Images: Miriam O'Connor, 2016. Courtesy of Sarah Browne and Jesse Jones.

deployed, and of their emotive and/yet analytical power (Figure 4.4; Browne and Jones 2016).[9]

The performances activated the visible and tangible—space, objects, documents and bodies—in multiple ways, too nuanced and complex to do justice here. For example, they were located in 'historically resonant spaces'—a hospital, a courtroom; they engaged 'objects of cultural significance'—such as a speculum used by police in the nineteenth century to forcibly examine women believed to be prostitutes for signs of venereal disease; and they used existing artefacts to inform the design of new ones (*In the Shadow of the State* website). In so doing, they drew attention to law's affective dimensions, its 'extra-textual' and 'material' effects, which tend to be 'resistant' and, indeed, 'experienced prior', to 'language and symbolization'; as well as, more specifically, to the false sense of control, predictability and universality that we tend to associate with legal agreements (Enright and Kinsell 2021, 7–9 and 15). Here I will focus on how the works made visible and tangible questions of sociolegal concern through the devices of archive and formal agreement.

In preparation for the performances, legal academic Máiréad Enright assembled an 'archive' of the 'contractual practices' of both state and non-state actors that affect the rights of women in the relevant jurisdiction. The archive was made available 'as a bound document or object for participants to peruse and discuss with mediators in advance of agreeing to participate' in the performance (Sarah Browne, Personal Communication, 23 March 2021. See further in Laws 2016). For the Dublin performance, the archive included a medical consent form that influenced the design of a 'Declaration of Consent'. Those wishing to participate fully in the performance were

asked to sign this 'hybrid document'—'part contract, part consent form'—
in order to gain entry (Enright and Kinsella 2021, 5). In London, the archive
included a Claimant Commitment Form, in exchange for the completion
of which participants received a 'voucher', based on a food bank voucher,
which entitled them entry to the performance. In each location, the contents of the Declaration were developed in a closed legal drafting workshop
involving 'performers, artists and organisers connected to the issues of the
project in each place' (Sarah Browne, Personal Communication, 23 March
2021). For example, the Declaration for the Dublin performance began:

> This is an Artistic Performance. The Performance will be [sic] begin
> with the sound of a triangle. You will be Touched by one or more female
> Performers, nominated by the Artists. That Touch will be improvised,
> direct and non-forceful. Performers will exercise their Discretion in
> deciding how to Touch you. However, the Touch(es) Administered may
> be experienced as having one or more of the following qualities …

> Significant, unavoidable or frequently occurring risks identified in
> the contract included, sensations of embarrassment (e.g. blushing,
> sweating, shaking); sensations of awkwardness, self-consciousness,
> nervousness, anxiety (e.g. giggling, digestive discomfort); feelings of
> bewilderment or boredom; interpretive difficulties; heightened arousal;
> sense of social difference highlighted through interpretation of perfor-
> mance (gender, age, class, sexuality, ethnicity); sense of anticlimax.
> Uncommon, but more serious risks included, outbursts of emotion
> (tears, rage, confusion, laughter); panic attacks; sense of accomplish-
> ment or empowerment; sense of powerlessness/impotence; onset of
> spontaneous civil disobedience; risk of radicalisation; hypersensitivity
> to the future touch of the State.

> (ArtAngel website)

Both the London and the Dublin documents included a 'touch wheel'
(Figure 4.5), which emphasized the consent-centred approach of the project as a whole—that is, it sought to capture not 'the intention of the per-
former' but rather 'how the touch may be received/experienced/interpreted'
by participants (Sarah Browne, Personal Communication, 23 March 2021).
Crucially, although the Declarations 'alluded to' *The Touching Contract*
itself, 'it was never fully identified'—nor indeed did many of the participants investigate, let alone query, the Declarations (Enright and Kinsella
2021, 5).

We can think of this as a speculative work that generates a practical-
critical-imaginative, structured-yet-free ecosystem in which participants

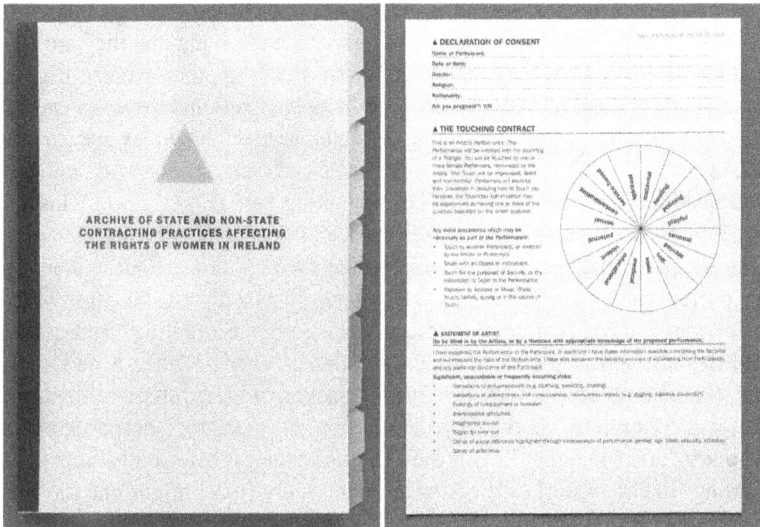

Figure 4.5 Designed artefacts supporting a performance of *The Touching Contract* in Dublin, 2016. An archive of contractual documents compiled by a legal expert (left) and the front page of a contract between the artists, Sarah Browne and Jesse Jones, and the participants. Designer Oonagh Young. Image: Miriam O'Connor, 2016. Courtesy of Sarah Browne and Jesse Jones.

can ask, among other things, what if we were to approach consent as an embodied concept, and from the perspective, and through the experiences, of those whose consent do we seek to obtain? It is also prefigurative in the sense that it invites participants to behave, for the moment, as if consent were already a concept that we were already willing and able effectively to discuss, to give and to receive, in everyday life, and to experience the risks and rewards, the liberations, the awkwardnesses, the indeterminacies, of such an imaginary.

To return to the wider proposition underpinning the present volume, we can ask: How, if at all, might the strategies deployed in *The Touching Contract*, in particular, the distinctive embodied practices drawn from performance arts, be applied to other fields of sociolegal concern, even—perhaps especially—those that are not directly concerned with bodies? And what might be the risks and rewards for research and research relations? '*The Touching Contract* as performed is diffuse and unpredictable' and 'makes no specific claim for change'. But it would be a mistake to conclude that it is therefore not capable of generating what I am framing in this volume as meaningful contributions. By placing textual, material and affective dimensions of law in a shared space—making them available to be 'read continuously with one another', without implying that they are one and the same, or that one is more important than the other, we can trigger an abductive 'flash of insight', because 'new connections' between, on the one hand, the languages of law and, on the other hand, how they are experienced, are made 'legible'. In this way, we can actively prompt and facilitate a 'transition' towards 'other ways of inhabiting law' (Enright and Kinsella 2021, 9, 11–2). Such insights and effects can occur not only within but also between participants. The interpersonal '*encounters*' that are 'provoked' by the performances can be seen as 'co-generate[ing] a dissensual community … of sense'—one that at once 'preserves incommensurability', indecision and dissent, and at the same time, 'anticipates or pre-figures a new reality'. Such communities may be 'fragile', lacking a 'deep' shared 'identity', a 'mere "vibration"' between a succession of spectators or participants who are "apart-together"'. But they can nevertheless afford a 'glimpse' or passing 'manifest[ion] of the kind of community [that] might one day be' (Enright and Kinsella 2021, 13).

To the extent that any sociolegal researcher, or community of researchers, seeks to keep the door open to understanding the legal as existing neither wholly 'inside' nor wholly 'outside' human perceptions, expectations and experiences, the embodied practices deployed in *The Touching Contract* offer enormous potential. Setting aside the extensive and long-running tangle of debates among social theorists, psychoanalysts and others over the precise distinctions between, and relative significance of, these internal and external dimensions of the world, both simply must be taken into account by those who wish to make and communicate a sense of law as a social phenomenon.

Four Legs Good

Jack Tan is an artist and former legal practitioner who 'uses law, social relations, and cultural norms to create video, performances, sculpture, and participatory projects that highlight the rules — customs, rituals, habits and theories — that guide human behaviour' (Tan 2020a, 23). As a law student, Tan had picked up on the Inuit tradition of the 'song duel', which 'involved community-based performance and singing as litigation' and aimed at 'conciliation' and 'humour' rather than 'blame' and 'formality'. His project *Karaoke Court* (2014–present) is an arbitration process and live performance in which 'participants select, prepare and perform songs as a way of resolving their disputes' before a judge and an audience of jurors (Ranjan Undated). Participants sign an arbitration contract to render the process and the decision legally binding. Each sitting of the Karaoke Court—there have been three to date—has been supported by designed emblems, leaflets and posters (Jack Tan website).

In 2018, Tan and collaborators created a fictitious Animal Justice Court for three days in the old Victorian courtroom at Leeds Town Hall. The project, entitled *Four Legs Good*, was part of the Leeds Compass Festival of 'live art and interactive encounters'. As in Karaoke Court, the intention of the project was not so much to create new art as to create new 'legal norms', and in particular to prompt and facilitate us to 'reconsider our understanding of the position of humans in relation to animals and the environment' (Jack Tan website).

The project generated structured-yet-free spaces for experts and members of the public to inhabit—a visible, tangible social world with processual, professional, cultural, material, temporal, spatial, normative and conceptual dimensions. Together with local animal charities, Tan co-designed a series of live 90-minute 'moot' trials, each complete with a live animal defendant—a dog facing charges of sheep-worrying, a band of invasive American signal crayfish charged with the mass murder of indigenous white-clawed crayfish—supported by human Animal Friends. In one case, *R v Snoopy*, a vulnerable sheep witness gave video-linked testimony as to her injuries from the safety of her farm so that she would be spared the anguish of being in the same room as her alleged 'worrier' (Figure 4.6). In each case, human legal professionals acting as barristers and judges, and a human jury drawn from members of the public, deliberated, decided and sentenced the accused animals. Video of the proceedings reveals an overall air of solemnity, albeit with the occasional moment of near playfulness (Tan 2020a).

Figure 4.6 Victim Ms Apple Meadowfoot (left) and Defendant Snoopy (right) give evidence in *R v Snoopy* as part of Jack Tan's work *Four Legs Good* commissioned for the Compass Festival 2018 in Leeds. Images © Lizzie Coombes 2018. Reproduced with permission.

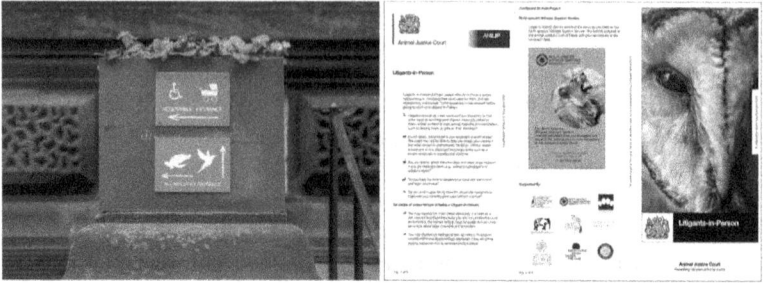

Figure 4.7 'Inclusive signage (left; Image: Lizzie Coombes 2018) and a foldable information leaflet for animals attending the Animal Justice Court as Litigants-in-Person (right; Image: Jack Tan). Both created as part of *Four Legs Good*, a work by Jack Tan, commissioned for the Compass Festival Leeds, 2018. Reproduced with permission.

The project was enhanced throughout by graphic design—this time expertly designed signage that referenced avian and reptile, alongside human, users; a court website; leaflets directed towards those appearing without a lawyer, with learning disabilities, who are minors; legal heritage displays; and an Annual Review of the Court (Figure 4.7. See Jack Tan website).[10] Few things are more practical than ensuring that users can find their way to a toilet or communicate their evidence to a court. To conjure these practicalities directly into the everyday is a critical and imaginative act.

It is perhaps the bright and elegant 'Annual Review', designed in collaboration with Dairus Ou, that establishes the most enduring legacy for the Court (Tan 2018). It begins with a foreword by the 'animal mayor' of Leeds and a message from the 'Presiding Judge of the AJC', both of which locate the 'Court' as part of the Leeds community, and of a long, more and less accommodating, history of animals in the law. The latter thread is picked up in a more detailed 'history' of animal justice, which begins in the truth of thirteenth-century medieval trials in which animals were treated as if (as opposed to 'as if') they were legal persons, and blends into the fictional establishment in 1918 of the contemporary Animal Justice Court. From there we move deep into an increasingly elaborate fiction. There are details of the three 'ground-breaking cases' heard in the live hearings, and an advertisement for the 'firm' Two Paws LLP 'supporting all creatures great and small since 1971', complete with the invitation to 'contact us via our Mycelium Network ID' (I leave to you the pleasure of Googling that one). The 'Animal Justice Court Research Unit' reports on its ongoing projects that analyse the operation of the Court, as well as wider investigations into alternative dispute resolution among animals, how to protect animals against the harvesting of their organs for use in humans and what the implications might be of allowing rivers, forests and so on to appear as litigants in the Court. Progress on legal education and accessibility is set out, including the introduction of a waterway to facilitate access for freshwater animals; animal-centred wayfinding signage and information leaflets; and an exhibition celebrating the heritage of the Animal Justice Court. Here there are especially regular and clear nods to (human) user-centred and inclusive dimensions of design, as well access to justice. A section is reserved to celebrate the 'Court community' including personnel: Jess, a mix-breed dog that volunteers as a 'Human Friend' to support humans throughout the court process; Bothie, a foxy, and therefore nocturnal, witness who was grateful to be able to attend night court to ease childcare constraints; Les, the estates and night-time manager who works to ensure the light is dimmed just right for those nocturnal sittings; and Andi, a solicitor at Two Paws LLP. The Report concludes with a summary of the support on offer from the Multi-Species Witness Support programme, of which Jess is a part including its Litigants-in-Person Project.

We can see *Four Legs Good* as a work of speculative service design—service design in the sense that meticulous attention was paid to the needs of the users of the court and their journey through it; speculative in the sense that animal courts do not exist today but their introduction is possible given that they have existed in the past; and because the idea of reconsidering relations between humans, animals and the environment, especially as constructed in law, has long been advocated by environmental and indigenous rights activists. We can also see it as a prefigurative work in the sense that it prompted and facilitated participants to move beyond speculatively asking 'what if' there were an Animal Justice Court and to behave prefiguratively 'as if' it already existed. But to what avail? 'Legal interpretation, Robert Cover wrote, takes places in a field of pain and death. These disappear where law is understood as immaterial; a set of abstract reasons, beyond touch' (Enright and Kinsella 2021, 22). Designed speculations and prefigurations can help us to 'mak[e] law palpable again' and generate 'the possibility empathetic response'—as opposed to mere 'reaction'—now and in the future (Enright and Kinsella 2021, 22). This observation is especially helpful in understanding the how and why *Four Legs Good* works to advance understandings of the relationships between law and animals. It is hard to consider in the abstract what it means to be held responsible, by the state and your peers, in a public forum; all the more so to do so empathetically—that is, in a way that is alert to the possibility, and then the actuality, of multiple perceptions, experiences and expectations. It is harder still to meaningfully consider this question in relation to animals. Tina Kinsella has coined the term 'affectosphere', meaning 'a transitive and relational senso-rium that provokes participants' capacity to be affected by traumatic legal history and to respond to it in transformative ways', to capture the space that is generated by *The Touching Contract* (Enright and Kinsella 2021, 3). We can think of Jan Tan's Animal Court as an affectosphere in which law, as it might be experienced by animals, is made palpable to humans.

Reflections

Designers can enhance our ability as researchers to bridge between pasts, presents and futures. Conventional design focuses on making new things for the future—artefacts, spaces, systems—and is judged by how 'ele-gantly' it resolves 'conflicts among aesthetics, production, usability and costs'. Such conflicts can only be resolved with reference to sociomaterial pasts and presents. Similarly, speculative design focuses on materializing abstract dimensions of alternative futures, but its success is measured by its ability 'simultaneously' to 'sit in this world, the here-and-now', and to 'belong to another yet-to-exist one' (Dunne and Raby 2013, 11, 43–4, 70 and 76). Any findings from the kinds of forensic, speculative and prefigura-tive interventions introduced previously are necessarily 'limited, situated and particular', and the impact of any emergent proposals will necessarily be 'bounded' (Di Salvo 2016, 34). But this is a limitation of all research, and one with which sociolegal researchers are familiar. So how else might sociolegal researchers work with designers to make such temporal bridges and make them more accessible and traversable? This is a thread that I am exploring in my ongoing work on law and island-wide economic life in Cyprus.

We can also think of design practitioners and their ways as offering alter-native, potentially transformative, visions of research relations. None of the experts mentioned in this chapter would, I hazard, embrace the designerly language of 'user-centredness'. But in all cases, a deep concern for, and close attention to, those who are in any way entangled with their work is palpable. In the words of Forensic Architecture's founding director and prin-cipal investigator, Eyal Weizman, 'No uninvolved investigator would have bothered to go to the lengths we have without being in solidarity with the victims whose truth is being undermined or denied' (Weizman 2017, 74); and Mariam Asad has proposed prefigurative design specifically as a way of securing 'research justice'—that is, better research relations and outcomes especially in collaborative community-based research (Asad 2019a, 200:1 and 200:9). If we think of sociolegal research as, like architecture, operating across three 'sites': The 'field' where the life of law is lived and from which we gather signs of that life; the 'studio' where we analyse what signs of life we have gathered and composed into arguments; and the 'forum' where those arguments are presented and challenged, we can ask, How might we use designerly ways to prompt and facilitate enrichments of and challenges to understandings across these three sites, and thereby make research relations more meaningful? This too is a thread that I am exploring in my ongoing work on law and island-wide economic life in Cyprus.

Notes

1 One source of such imaginaries has been the Feminist Judgements project instigated by Rosemary Hunter, Clare McGlynn and Erika Rackley (2010), which has, in turn, inspired, for example, the Wild Law Judgement project (Rogers and Maloney 2017).

2 For instance, we will see that the practice of Forensic Architecture exploits, among other things, the visual power of the grid (see Roberts and Thrift 2002), and the practices of Sarah Browne, Jesse Jones and Jack Tan exploit, among other things, the semiotic power of official signs and symbols and spaces (see Crow 2003).

3 The 'emergence' of Forensic Architecture can be seen as part of the wider material or, more specifically, 'forensic turn' in which our 'attention has shifted ... to narratives led by things, traces, objects and algorithms'. The turn began with the identification of Josef Mengele's bones in Argentina and the 'culture of testimony' developed by Holocaust survivors at the trial of Adolf Eichmann, and has been amplified by diverse trends such as, for example, 'philosophical movements such as object-oriented ontologies' and 'forensic crime series on television' (Weizman 2017, 78-80 and 83).

4 For example, for many years, the resolution of satellite imagery released to the public remained at 0.5 metres per pixel—not for any technical reasons, but thanks to a political decision, given legal force, to ensure that human figures would remain undetected (Weizman 2017, 28-30).

5 In their investigation *Triple Chaser*, they went further, collecting images of a particular type of tear gas canister in multiple natural and simulated settings and using them to generate a 'machine learning and computer vision workflow' through which they, and human rights activists, can automatically identify when those canisters appear in new digital images (Forensic Architecture website).

6 See the Business and Human Right Resource Centre KiK Law Suit website for updates on the case.

7 For videos introducing embodied methodologies, see Kieft (2020).

8 *In the Shadow of the State* was commissioned by Create and Artangel. Supported by ART: 2016, the Arts Council's programme as part of Ireland 2016, the centenary of the Easter Rising in the Republic of Ireland, Dublin City Council and Heart of Glass (St. Helen's). For a full list of production credits for each element of the project, see *In the Shadow of the State* website.

9 The film 'Touching Contract 2016' (Browne and Jones 2016) was produced by Artangel, co-commissioner of the project, and was shot by Kate McDonough.

10 There is even a scholarly fiction in the form of a chapter in an edited collection that introduces the Animal Justice Court and is ostensibly contributed by Jess the dog (Tan 2020a).

5   Entering design mode

This chapter sets out a series of tasks intended to prompt and facilitate sociolegal researchers to enter into design mode. We can think of them as sociolegal design briefs. Each is designed to promote problem solving and/ or sense-making through being practical-critical-imaginative, experimentation and making things visible and/or tangible. Many involve speculating about 'what if', and/or acting prefiguratively 'as if'. Most can be used to enhance multiple dimensions of research—empirical, conceptual, normative, processual, relational; and across multiple stages—conceptualisation, data gathering, analysis, communication and reflection. Although designed and tested primarily with sociolegal ways in mind, most of the briefs will have something to offer researchers from the wider social sciences and humanities. They are best completed together, or at least in communication, with one or more others—a fellow researcher, whether or not they are working on the same project, a supervisor, a fellow research student or a non-expert critical friend. But any resulting reflections can just as well be kept entirely private, for example, in a sketchbook, as shared informally via tweets and/or blogs or in formal publications. Finally, these briefs can be used in formal research methodology training, each one to be completed in relation to the students' own research projects in an iterative process of learning-by-doing.[1]

The practical barriers to operating in design mode are easily surmounted: Gather together some standard office supplies such as thick black felt tip pens, glue, scissors, large paper, adhesive putty and sticky notes; some unwanted second-hand plastic animal figures and building blocks from family, colleagues and friends; and, if you have access to funds, some malleable materials such as clay, especially the types that can be air-dried. Identify a room with big tables and blank walls that you can treat as a pop-up studio when the mood takes you (see also Stickdorn et al. 2018a, 430–42).

DOI: 10.4324/9780367177683-5

A greater challenge to overcome is the fact that by the time we reach adulthood, many of us have lost our creative confidence (James and Brookfield 2014, 58), whether through lack of use or because it has been actively quashed. This loss of confidence matters because being in design mode involves creating things—making imaginaries visible and tangible. So, the briefs are designed to re-instil it—to activate what Audre Lorde has described, specifically in celebration of Black lesbian women, as 'places of possibility within' that 'are ancient and hidden', that 'have survived and grown strong through darkness' (1984, 36–7)—and direct them towards research.

Perhaps the most difficult challenge associated with entering design mode is to avoid ending up with a 'fragmented', fascination-driven selection of strategies that is not 'embed[ded]' within a wider methodology (Mannay 2016, 85 and 95). Each of the briefs set out in this chapter can be approached as one-off experiments, and that may be all that some are willing or able to attempt in the first instance. But the need to integrate ad hoc methodological adventures into the wider whats, whys and hows is inevitable. The first set of briefs on 'prototyping' is designed, among other things, to prompt and facilitate you to do just that.

Finally, courage. As much as interdisciplinary work can be 'wonderfully energizing', it can also be 'extremely tiring' (James and Brookfield 2014, 209), and even make you (feel) a fool. There is inherent value in 'queer use'—that is, the use of something 'by those for whom', or for a purpose which 'it was not intended' and repeated such 'use can make use less queer' (Ahmed 2019, 34–5 and 44), and indeed, its very queerness may itself be cause for celebration. But when you decide to enter a new disciplinary sphere, you enter a form of 'exile'—not only in the sense that 'you are always going to be marginal', but also in the sense that, since there is no 'prescribed path', much of 'what you do … has to be made up'. The secret, advised Edward Said (1994), is to 'experience that fate not as a deprivation', or 'to be bewailed' but rather 'as a sort of freedom, a process of discovery in which you do things according to your own pattern' (Said 1994, 62). So aim not to do 'what one is supposed to do'. Rather, 'ask why one does it, who benefits from it' and 'how can it reconnect with a personal project and original thoughts'. Adopt the 'spirit' of 'an amateur' who 'can enter and transform the merely professional routine most of us go through into something much more lively and radical' (Said 1994, 62 and 82–3).

The following briefs are divided into three sections: Prototyping a project (Briefs 1–7); Thinking through the material world (Briefs 8–10); and

Thinking through the visual world (Briefs 11–15). Some are accompanied by reflections of participants who have tested them with me over the years during ad hoc events or formal learning settings (see Chapters 1 and 3).

Prototyping a project

At the heart of any research project there (ought to) lie three questions: What are you researching? How are you researching it? Why (including for whom) are you researching it? The answers to these questions will not always be clear, and they will shift over time, because your research process and the real world that you are researching are 'wicked'—that is, open, complex, dynamic and networked (Chapter 1). So you need to work iteratively and provisionally towards answers that are individually and collectively coherent. This set of briefs is designed to make that work more possible and probable.

Brief 1: Outlining

Albert Einstein is credited with arguing that, given an hour to solve a problem, he would spend the first 55 minutes identifying what question to ask 'for once I know the proper question I could solve the problem in five minutes'. As Sundhya Pahuja puts it, our aim ought to be 'to construct questions' that 'challenge the reader's taken-for-granted assumptions'. To do this, we need to construct questions that are 'bendy'—for example, 'What relations does a particular law or norm create and with what effect', rather than 'straight'—for example, 'Does a particular law or norm meet its stated objective' (2021, 10 of 16). This brief is designed[2] to help you to surface the questions that do/will underpin your project, to assess their quality and understand how they fit together, both internally and in relation to the wider field, and where necessary, to improve them. You are also invited to develop the habit of zooming in and out of it, as well as reshaping it, on a regular basis.

Process

Watch 'Powers of Ten' (1977), a film by designers Ray Eames and Charles Eames in which the field of vision, which centres on a picnic in a park, systematically zooms to ten times farther out every ten seconds before reversing to zoom in at the same rate. Over the course of nine minutes, we see the same scene from well beyond our galaxy, right down to the level of a DNA molecule within a white blood cell. At all times we know where we are and where we were, and we can anticipate where we are going.

Set aside any existing notes, outlines or sources, and generate a Dynamic Outline for your current or future research project:

- Write your main research question at the top of a sheet of unlined paper (landscape orientation).
- Note down the sub-questions that you must, as a matter of pure logic, address in order to answer your main research question. Generate as many as you can. Scatter them across the whole sheet.
- Note down answers of one or two words under each question.
- Identify the logical order in which to address the questions and number them accordingly.
- Photograph the outcome for your records.

Next, transpose your ordered sub-questions into a word-processing file.

- Under each sub-question include the brief answers, and indicate what the sources—for example, literature, statistics and interview transcripts—you intend to use to generate answers.
- Add an additional layer of hierarchy to the outline by formatting your sub-questions with the built-in heading styles from your word-processing software (see Rado undated).

Your outline is now a living document through which you can explore and restructure your argument. In Outline View:

- Zoom into each question and assess whether it could be improved. For example, is it just a 'straight line question', or is it a 'bendy' one (Pahuja 2021).
- Zoom out a little to see the balance of the piece—where do you have more and less material, including sources.
- Zoom out more to test the flow of your argument from sub-question to sub-question.
- Drag and drop sub-questions to new locations as appropriate.

Notice that you can convert this document directly into your article/chapter/thesis/book. By answering each of your sub-questions in turn, you will eventually complete the piece. Everything that your write will be relevant because each sub-question has emerged from your main research question. And as your research question evolves, so you can adjust each sub-question and incrementally shift your argument. Just before completing your piece of writing, you can convert each sub-question into a more engaging heading.

Brief 2: Proposing

Figure 5.1 Postgraduate research students exhibiting and critiquing a weekly brief during the Research Methods on Law module, Autumn 2019, Kent Law School. Image Amanda Perry-Kessaris.

This brief is designed to help you capture on a single page every dimension of your research—empirical, conceptual, normative, processual, relational; and every phase of your research project —conceptualisation, data gathering, analysis, communication, reflection—of your research project on a single page. This will allow you to test the coherence of your project, share and compare it with others and track how your project changes over time.

Process

Set aside all your notes and sources. Generate a Research Proposition by answering the following questions on one side of A4:

- What is your research question?
- How will you go about answering it?
- What do you expect the answers to be?
- What problems do you anticipate?
- Why is your research meaningful for academics and the wider world?

Print out the resulting summary and stick it on a wall. If you are working with a group, line all the propositions up along the wall and compare each element across the group.

Later, keep your proposition up on your own wall to serve as a constant reference point, reality check and source of comfort. Repeat this process at regular intervals. Track your progress between versions.

Check your Dynamic Outline (Brief 1) against your Research Proposition (Brief 2) to test whether they fit together. Update both documents regularly, especially immediately after completing any other briefs so that you can capture what you have learned.

Participant reflection

> [This process] was excruciating, but once done, it was liberating to see that it all made some sense.
>
> (Elena Paris 2020)

Brief 3: Prefiguring

This brief is designed to help you to prefigure your research journey, to act as if you were moving through it so that you can prepare yourself for what lies ahead.

Figure 5.2 Postgraduate research students walking the labyrinth at the start of the
Research Methods in Law module, October 2019, University of Kent.
Image: Amanda Perry-Kessaris.

Process

Explore 'Mountains of Metaphor', an illustrated interactive digital map by
Clare Williams (Undated) of her journey towards a PhD in law, completed
against the odds.

Choose a labyrinth.

• You can either visit a labyrinth; download and trace an image of a labyrinth with your finger or complete a virtual labyrinth online. For help
with each option, visit the Labyrinth Society website, which includes
a labyrinth locator, a downloadable template and a virtual tour, or the
Labyrinths in Britain website.
• Note that unlike mazes, labyrinths 'have a single path, low or no walls and
are straightforward to walk', so they emphasize intuition and imagination
rather than problem solving (James and Brookfield 2014, 129–32).[3]

Move slowly through your chosen labyrinth looking up, down and around
as you go. As you move, ask yourself:

• What activities will you undertake at each stage of your research
process?

- With whom will you interact? How?
- How will you feel at the beginning, middle and end?
- How will the research process change you? Your field of study?
- In what ways do you expect your experience to differ from that of a doctrinal legal researcher? A non-legal researcher?
- What have you learned about what lies ahead?

Participant reflection

> Seeing the 'end in sight' but seeing it 'moving away' made me think about how I will feel in the coming years, thinking the research is finally taking shape and then realising I am still a long way out. It was the first time since submitting the proposal that I thought about what I was going to be doing at each stage, and what may change during the life of the project. It has helped me to prepare for 'unexpected turns'. I realised that this new community could be a source of friendship, support and encouragement.
>
> (Wilfred Chitembwe 2020)

Brief 4: 3D Modelling

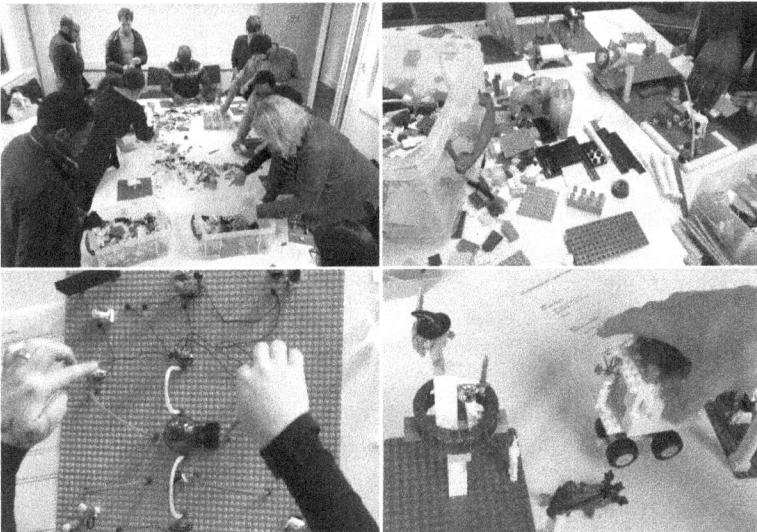

Figure 5.3 Postgraduate research students building and sharing 3D models of their research during the Research Methods on Law module, Spring 2018 and 2019, Kent Law School. Images: Amanda Perry-Kessaris.

When you do something 'with fingers first, rather than designing in your head then building' you work kinaesthetically, 'thinking through your fingers' (James and Brookfield 2014, 116). This brief is designed to show how we can use our hands, including in the absence of sight, to draw ourselves incrementally outwards from the practical, to the practical-critical, to the practical-critical-imaginative.

Process

Watch: 'Sociolegal Model-Making 1: Decision', a film available at vimeo. com/amandaperrykessaris.

Use a modular building system such as LEGO—or if that is not possible then, for example, use a pack of index cards annotated with text and/or images and some pieces of string—to complete the following three builds. Try to work with a partner who can interact with you and with your model (see Chapter 2). In each case, photograph and then narrate the model, recording yourself to listen back later:

- Make an explanatory model of your project in which you include representations of relatively abstract elements such as key concepts and lines of enquiry, and relatively concrete elements such as key actors and locations, as well as the relationships between these elements.
- Add a representation of yourself into the model, focusing on where you see yourself in relation to the project. You might highlight relatively abstract aspects of that relationship, such as your normative position in relation to key themes; and/or relatively concrete aspects of that relationship, such as how much you have yet to do. In so doing, you might reveal to yourself, in particular in discussion with others, why you have taken one approach rather than another, or why you are taking so much or so little time over a particular aspect of your research and what are the risks and rewards.
- Adapt the model to show where you and your project might be in the future. You might include, for example, challenges and solutions, nightmares and fantasies, certainties and indeterminacies.
- Consider: What elements of your project and relationships between those elements have been made visible, or more visible or differently visible through this process? Your relationship to your project? Your project as it was, is and might yet be?

Participant reflection

> [It] helped me not to get too attached ... the Lego pieces can quickly be moved or dismantled if a new idea emerges thereby freeing me to experiment with new concepts.
>
> (Wilfred Chitembwe 2020)

> [A] second year PGR student asked me where was I in relation to my thesis. This was something I had not previously thought about, except that I was the outside observer of the spectacle of the world ... keeping myself aside from the fight. ... I represented myself in a boat, that is 'grounded' in the floating waters of legal indeterminacy, again loosely connected every now and then to one or another provisional and contingent ground that could be laid from time to time in support of assertions ... Retrospectively, I would have placed myself amidst the various foundations to signal that I was involved, that I was part of the story I was telling, which concerned me too.
>
> (Elena Paris 2020)

> [It] was a way to make [my project] enjoyable but also understandable ... to other academics but especially to non-academics. [In the] process, I had to clarify some ideas to myself. I shared [a photo] with my mum and friends.
>
> (Elena Caruso 2020)

Brief 5: Personas

This brief invites you to develop a sense of the people at the centre of your research by developing a set of 'personas'—that is, 'rich descriptions', each one of 'a specific fictional person' that can reasonably and usefully be treated 'as an archetype exemplifying a group of people' (Stickdorn et al. 2018b, 69). You can generate a persona at any stage of your research process and you can refine them over time. Early attempts will help to highlight biases and blind spots, both in your own approach and in the wider literature. If you iteratively refine personas over time, you will generate a record of early misconceptions and ever-deepening insights. Note that it can be especially useful to generate personas alongside journey maps and system maps (see Chapter 2; Stickdorn 2018a, 41–2, b, 69–72).

Process

Watch 'All that we share', a film by TV 2 Danmark (2017), available on YouTube.

List all the categories of person that will appear in your research—for example, businesspeople, bureaucrats, consumers, activists, judges—or, if your work is relatively abstract, you might, for example, be focusing on commentators or academics.

- Choose at least three categories of person to focus on in detail.

Visit the personas page available under 'tools' on the Development Impact and You (DIY) website at diytoolkit.org.

- Watch the short video and download the Persona worksheet template.

Gather all available information about each of your three chosen categories of person, including your own primary data, secondary data from academic and policy literature, documentaries, podcasts, message boards, newspapers and so on.

- Consider: Along what dimensions is it meaningful, in the context of your research, to distinguish between different types of people who might fall within one of your categories?

Complete two DIY Persona worksheets for each of your three chosen categories of person (six worksheets in total), each representing a different type of person that falls within the same category. In completing the worksheet, your aim is to adopt the character of that idealized person and look back through their eyes at your research—the questions you are asking, the sources you are using, the assumptions you are making, the methods you are using and so on.

Place the worksheets next to each other on a table or wall.

- Consider: What additional information do you need about each of these people in order to place them conceptually, empirically, normatively and processually within your research? How can you find it?

- Note: The aim is not to assume or pretend that you know the answers, but rather to imagine what the answers might be; to think about the significance of any gaps for various stages of your research; and to consider how you can go about resolving/addressing those gaps in ways that are respectful of, and not burdensome to, those who wish to understand.

Extensions:

- Generate personas representing the academic users of your research. What do they think they need? How can you give them what they need or convince them that they need what you can give?
- Download and complete a stakeholder and public analysis template and/or impact planning template from the Fast Track Impact website (see also Reed 2018). This template will help you to identify, for example, how interested different stakeholders and publics are likely to be in your research; whether they are likely to ignore, help or hinder you; and how you can make your work be, and be recognized as, more helpful to those stakeholders and publics, as well as reduce the chance that they impede your progress .

Brief 6: Reverse engineering

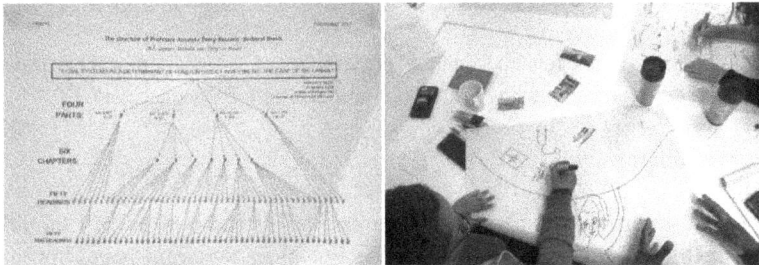

Figure 5.4 'Reverse engineering' brief Part 1 (left) and Part 2 (right) completed by students on the Research Methods in Law module, Autumn 2017 and 2018, Kent Law School. Images: Amanda Perry-Kessaris.

This brief is designed to prompt and facilitate you to expose and confront how an extended, written sociolegal argument can 'succeed' or 'fail' to make a meaningful contribution.[4]

Process

Watch 'The craft of writing effectively', a seminar delivered by Larry McNerney (2014) and available on YouTube. Note: As Larry McNerney himself acknowledges, many will baulk at thinking about writing in this utilitarian way, but most will nevertheless recognize the powerful truth at the heart of his argument.

- Consider: Whose thinking and/or behaviour do you wish to change when you are writing about, speaking about or otherwise sharing your research?

Choose an existing sociolegal work that is of special interest to you—whether substantively or stylistically, whether you hope to emulate or challenge it:

- Read the abstract, introduction and conclusion, as well as the table of contents if available.
- Establish the anatomy of the work by counting headings, subheadings, words, footnotes and images, and by identifying key dates, places, people, events, organizations/institutions and concepts.
- In a few words, capture the tone of the work.
- Consider: Whose thinking and/or behaviour does the work seem to want to change? What strategies does it use to achieve that aim? What more could it do?

Using a thick black felt tip pen and (preferably) an A2 sheet of paper, draw a visual summary capturing what you have learned about the work.

Participant reflection

> I start to reflect … about my potential readers and how much I should take care of them. How? By respecting their time and being honest [from] the beginning about the findings and directions of the 'journey' that I will propose in my writing. … [T]he ability to communicate law also has a *political* significance. It makes law a democratic discipline, something that anyone could understand and approach.
>
> (Elena Caruso 2020)

Brief 7: Refreshing

Answer the following questions at speed, focusing on your research project. Use a timer to make sure you spend no more than two minutes on each one:[5]

- Why this research? Why now?
- What three keywords would you use to explain your project to yourself?
- What three keywords would you use to explain your project to someone who knows nothing about it?
- Has anything in your research surprised you?
- Has anything in your research changed your mind?
- What is the most unusual source that you have used for your research?
- Who would you most like to talk to about your research?
- What is the most striking idea that you have come across during your research?
- What idea have you found impossible to understand?
- Which person, event, place or piece of writing has most informed your research?
- If you could put your project in a specific real-world location, where would you choose?
- What is your favourite quote that you have used to date?

Thinking through the material world

To research through the material world is to promote an 'active', as opposed to incidental, 'engagement with the capacities' of the material world 'to make methods provocative'. In order to access those capacities effectively, we must distinguish between different aspects of the material world, especially materials, things and objects, as well as the assemblages in which they may be entangled, whether by systematic collection or happenstance (Woodward 2020, 2 and 12). This set of briefs is designed to prompt and facilitate you to make considered use of each.

Brief 8: Materials

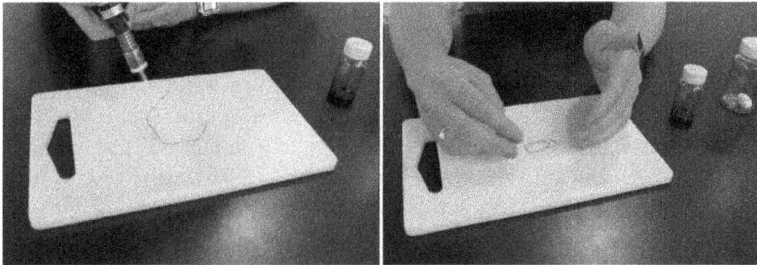

Figure 5.5 Zoe Laughlin performs a shape memory alloy at the UCL Institute of Making, August 2016. Images: Amanda Perry-Kessaris and Andy Renmei.

To research through materials is to focus on their properties as materials. For example, the material properties of water are such that, depending on the amount of energy contained in its atomic bonds, it may take the form of solid ice, liquid or steam. So, political theorist Jane Bennett (2010) has drawn attention to the 'vibrancy' inherent in materials. To think in terms of materiality is to contextualise the material in the wider world by emphasising how their properties 'can lead to materials having particular effects' (Woodward 2020, 17). For example, depending on its form, water will either freeze, wet or burn that with which it comes into contact. So, anthropologist Tim Ingold has drawn attention to the ongoing processes of making through which humans and materials come to be in evolving 'correspondence' with each other (Ingold 2013, 103–5). This brief is designed to prompt and facilitate you to correspond with vibrant materials to advance any aspect of your own research. It builds on the experiments conducted with Zoe Laughlin, using materials from the Institute of Making Materials Library, which were introduced in Chapter 3.

Process

Watch two films—'Materials-based gaze: An interview with Zoe Laughlin' and 'Sociolegal model-making 5: Material metaphoricization'—both available via vimeo.com/amandaperrykessaris.

Explore the online collection of the UCL Materials Library (Institute of Making website) using the 'selection', 'categories', 'state' and 'curiosities' tabs. Choose three materials to explore in depth:

- Why did you choose those materials?
- How do they relate to each other?
- What dimensions of your research do you feel are, or could with additional experimentation be, materialized in or through your collection? Consider in particular the conceptual, empirical, normative, analytical, processual and relational dimensions of your research.

Look for materials with similar properties in your immediate surroundings and try to perform and narrate them with your own hands and voice—note that you can acquire small quantities of some of the materials in the Library, for example, 'memory' wire and ferrofluid, from specialist suppliers (see Mindsets website):

- What new language—vocabulary, grammar—has this process prompted and facilitated you to develop for communicating about your research? What substantive insights? Has it reinforced existing language or insights?

- How exactly might you use this language and/or insights to enhance the meaningfulness of your research and/or research relations in future?

Brief 9: Things

Figure 5.6 Cigarette pack adapted by Paulo Vargiu (left) to highlight the risks of investor-state dispute resolution systems; and potato adapted by the author (right) to highlight the potential implications of understanding potatoes grown anywhere on the island of Cyprus as Cypriot. Images: Amanda Perry-Kessaris.

'Artefacts do not exist in a vacuum'. They are grounded in the materials and maker that made them, and the social relations of which they form a part. Furthermore, our interpretations of them are grounded in our wider social, including cultural, context (Mannay 2016, 46 and 63). For example, Gillian Rose (2016) proposes that visual and material meaning are made not only in the 'site' of the object itself but also in the sites of its production, of its circulation and of its 'audiencing'. So although expert analysis of visual and material culture is beyond the scope of this volume, it is always important to consider the circumstances under which a thing has been produced, distributed and used, and, in the case of a museum context, by whom and how it was collected, curated, exhibited and interpreted.

In this context, it can be useful to think of things, objects and assemblages as existing on a spectrum, and of their place on that spectrum being determined at least in part by how we humans relate to them. We can think of 'things' as always in a process of 'becoming', affecting and affected by use and context. Examples include cutlery, cars and trees. Then we can think of objects, such as an ornament, which are things that we can see and perhaps even touch, but which are fundamentally separate from or 'against' us (Ingold 2013, 85. See also Brown 2001; Sudjic 2008). Finally, we can think of those objects being gathered into a museum or gallery context— where they are classified as artefacts, because they have been created or adapted by humans, or as specimens, because they are natural (Hanan and Longair, 8. See also Candlin and Guins 2009)—and thereby becoming part of a formal assemblage or collection.

This brief is designed to prompt and facilitate you to draw on everyday things to advance any aspect of your research. Objects and assemblages are dealt with in more detail in the next brief.

Process

Read 'Mind in matter: An introduction to material culture theory and method' (Prown 1982).

Watch two films—'Reading an object: description deduction speculation', which is an audio recording of a 'reading' of a calliper; and 'Standard', a film inspired by my reading of the calliper. Both are available at vimeo.com/amandaperrykessaris.[6]

Explore three projects: the Planet Money T-shirt project (NPR 2013a and 2013b), A History of the World in 100 Objects (BBC 2010) and Stuff the British Stole (ABC 2021).

Identify a thing that plays a role in the sociolegal world that you are researching. 'Read' it using the technique set out in Prown (1982):

- Description: What can you observe through substantive analysis—for example, dimensions, colour, texture; content analysis—for example, are there any representations, decorations or text; and formal analysis—for example, what is its overall visual character? Make a sketch of it or capture its surface texture by rubbing a crayon or pencil on a sheet of paper you have laid over it.

- Deduction: What senses, ideas and emotions are generated when using or otherwise physically interacting with the thing or object or, in the case of an image, by imagining yourself into the world that it depicts.

- Speculation: Imagine the object, thing or image as a representation of some aspect of your research—empirical, conceptual, normative, processual, relational. First, look at the thing through the lens of your project. What conceptual, empirical, normative or processual aspects of your research are manifested in the thing? Look at your project through the lens of the thing. Is there any aspect of your research that you now see is well-expressed, or incomplete or missing? Aim for a 'free association of ideas and perceptions tempered only, and then not too quickly, by … common sense and judgment as to what is even vaguely plausible' (Prown 1982, 10).

Consider: How can you use this thing, and your reading of it, in different phases of your research—conceptualization, data gathering, analysis, communication, reflection?

Brief 10: Objects and assemblages

This brief prompts and facilitates you to draw both on an object and on its context to advance any aspect of your research, and, by extension, to consider museum collections as potential 'laboratories for rethinking society, places for showing … what is yet to exist' (Dunne and Raby 2013, 154).[7]

Process

Watch three films: First 'Sociolegal model-making 7: Object-based commentary in a curated space', a film documenting the Legal Objects workshop held at the British Museum (see Chapter 3) available at vimeo.com/amandaperrykessaris. Then 'Untold Narratives: Colonialism in natural history', a film by UCL Department of Science and Technology Studies (2020) which introduces the 'Displays of Power' exhibition at the Grant Museum of Zoology and 'Untitled', a poem written by Yomi Sode (2019) in response to that exhibition, both available via YouTube.

Explore the Pop-Up Museum of Legal Objects, which is available under 'collections' at amandaperrykessaris.org; and any other collection, museum or gallery, either in person or online.

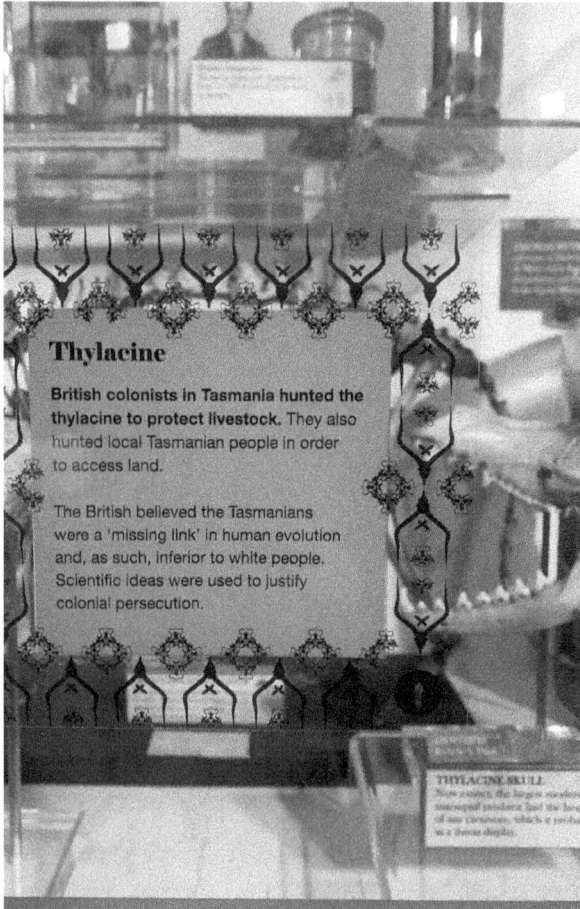

Figure 5.7 Temporary label overlaid on a permanent display case holding a specimen of a Tasmanian Thylacine in order to surface the threads of racism and empire that run through a natural history collection. 'Displays of Power: A Natural History of Empire'. Exhibition, Grant Museum of Zoology, 19 September 2019 to 21 June 2021, London. Image: Amanda Perry-Kessaris.

Choose an artefact or specimen:

- 'Read' it using the describe, deduce, speculate method set out previously.
- How did the object come to be part of this collection? What now exists in the places where it used to be?

- Who is curating this object? Why and for whom are they, or ought to be, curating it? Who in addition to you is, or ought to be, interpreting this object?
- How is the object arranged in relation to other objects in the collection? What connections are created, highlighted and erased?
- What techniques and technologies are associated with its display and interpretation? For example, do they prompt and facilitate widespread and user-led engagement?

Consider: How might you use this object, and your extended reading of it in different phases of your research—conceptualisation, data gathering, analysis, communication, reflection? Would you like to submit an object-based commentary to the Pop-up museum of legal objects? Would you like to create your own collection or assemblage?

Participant reflection

In a sense, the object acts as an anchor to reality—stopping [us] drifting off in a tide of dry, academic discussion, by tethering it to something we can not only see, but feel, approach and assess. It does more than that though. [I]t provides a point of entry for accessing the same content from different perspectives … [Y]ou can venture off along myriad paths around and of the object, [and then] compare and contrast those different pathways from … the shared starting point.

(Anonymous)

Thinking through the visual world

Designers hone their visual literacy by, for example, actively looking at their everyday surroundings for evidence of visual and material thinking and practice, and maintaining sketchbooks to document the evolving set of influences and observations that are shaping their ideas (James and Brookfield 2014, 69–92. See Figure 1.1 in Chapter 1). These briefs are designed to prompt and facilitate you to recognize and enhance your existing visual literacy, first, as a reader and producer of text and images; and then as a viewer and producer of combinations of text and image.[8] Note that the line between the visual and the material is always blurry, all the more so when, as in some of the following briefs, 'images are not just understood visually in terms of image composition and content but also as objects that are printed, stored and displayed' (Woodward 2020, 134).

Brief 11: Letter as form

This brief is designed to prompt and facilitate you to consider the extent to which the meaning of a word can be constructed, emphasized, altered and so on through the form of the letters from which it is made.

Process

First watch Helvetica' by Gary Hustwit (2007) available via hustwit.com. Note: It is long, intensely nerdy, and startlingly focused on the thinking and practice of white men based in Europe and the US; but it offers a solid point of departure.

Over the course of a week or so:

- Photograph or cut out the letters L l, A a and W w wherever and whenever you find them.
- Working digitally and/or with paper, construct the word law in as many ways as you find productive.

Consider:

- What factors—visual, social, cultural, economic, material and so on—render letterforms relatively 'neutral', such as those that make up the Helvetica typeface, as opposed to relatively 'expressive', such as those that you may have found in your visual research this week?
- What are the risks and rewards of choosing to work with relatively neutral or relatively expressive letterforms?
- If you had the freedom to choose, would you present the word law in a relatively neutral or a relatively expressive way when sharing your research? Why? What does this tell you about your relationship with law? With the potential users of your research?
- How might your future reading of legal and sociolegal texts be influenced by completing this brief?

Brief 12: Text as image

This brief is designed to emphasize the visual dimensions of sociolegal texts, to reveal how we can think with text and to show how, by manipulating text, we can promote different meanings. 'Typography is what language looks like' (Lupton 2010). When designers select typefaces and plan compositions, they draw on a combination of expert technical skills and cultural knowledge (Elam 2004, 2007; Kane 2013; Baines and Haslam 2012). For example, they draw on the fact that words communicate a greater or lesser

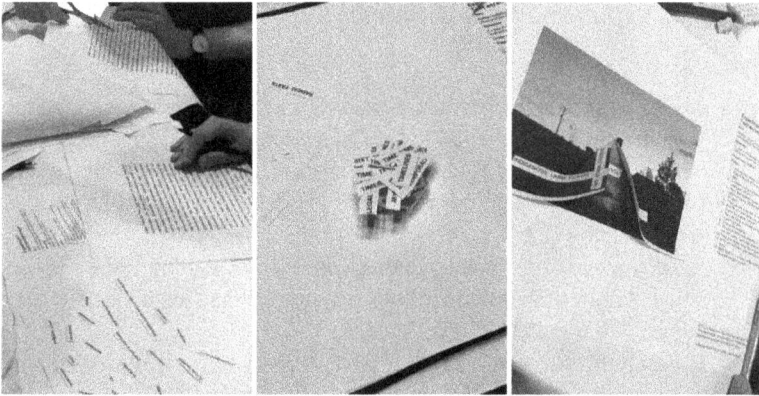

Figure 5.8 Examples of text and/as image completed by participants as part of the plenary session of '"New" legal temporalities: Discipline and resistance across domains of time', a conference organized by Emily Grabham and Sian Beynon-Jones as part of their AHRC-funded 'Regulating Time' networking project, September 2016. Images: Amanda Perry-Kessaris.

significance in a hierarchy of ideas depending on whether they are set to a relatively large or small scale, or bold or light weight; as well as whether they are placed to the top, left, right or bottom of a page. And they draw on the fact that any typeface—for example, even the familiar shapes of Times New Roman, Helvetica and Comic Sans carry with them a wealth of cultural subtext to which most readers are, albeit subconsciously, well-attuned. But there is more: Designers draw on the fact that typographic processes can help us to think (Lupton 2010).

Process

Watch 'Typographic Hierarchy', a film by Tony Pritchard (2010) available via Vimeo.

Choose a quotation that is important for your research. It might be from an interview or from a secondary source or from your own writing. Enter it into a word-processing document in Helvetica font (as we have seen, it is simple and common, therefore relatively neutral to many eyes) and double line spacing. Format the quotation in four different versions:

- 1 × 14 point font size, bold weight; 1 × 14 point font size, normal weight
- 1 × 28 point font size, bold weight; 1 × 28 point font size normal weight

Print all four versions onto A4 paper. Cut up the text into individual words or phrases. Lay the text out on another sheet of paper, ideally A3. Look at it as if it were an image:

- Try to encourage a particular reading of the quotation by working with the size, weight and location of the text on the page.
- Notice how you are forced to really look at, and weigh the significance of, each word, as well as its relationships with all the other words. Take a photo.
- Reset the quotation to encourage an alternative reading. Take a photo.
- What words have fallen by the wayside? What meaning has been gained and lost in the process?
- How might you use what you have learned to communicate about your research to others, for example, in posters and presentations, blog posts or formal publications?

Brief 13: Text and image

This brief is designed to show how by combining text with images, we can both promote alternative meanings and fix specific meanings. The distinction between words and images is not sharp: 'There can be no picture, it could be argued, that cannot also be read, and no written text that cannot be looked at' (Ingold 2013, 129). Furthermore, we can combine images and text together to fix and reinforce particular meanings. For example, collage is a familiar 'every-day material practice'. It involves 'cutting', 'altering' and 'combining' often 'disparate' 'images/materials', thereby making 'connections and contrasts'. These 'material, tangible and embodied' processes can generate 'findings' that may be 'surprising', but also 'ambiguous' and/or 'uncertain' (Woodward 2020, 70–1). One way to make collage more designerly—that is, to access and nurture not only its imaginative but also its practical and critical, potential—is to combine images and text.

Process

Watch 'What can graphic design reveal about law', a film (2014) available at vimeo.com/amandaperrykessaris.

Return to the quotation your were working on in Brief 12.

- Place the original version and your preferred layout in front of you.
- Select at least two keywords from the quotation and use them to search for an image online.

- Choose at least one image that is 'concrete'—that is, it depicts something identifiable; and one that is 'abstract'—that is, does not depict an identifiable thing. Print them out.

- Experiment with different combinations of images and text, cutting them up if necessary. Take photos of each arrangement. Note the alternative meanings you are producing. Fix your preferred layout with glue.

- How might you use what you have learned to communicate about your research to others, for example, in posters and presentations, blog posts or formal publications?

Extension: If you are organizing an event on a defined theme, print out all the abstracts and invite participants to fulfil this brief together at the beginning of the event using the words from those abstracts. Then distribute a selection of images and invite participants to combine the quotations and images. For an example in action watch 'Sociolegal model making 4: Discussion', a film available via vimeo.com/amandaperrykessaris .

Brief 14: Text and image into object

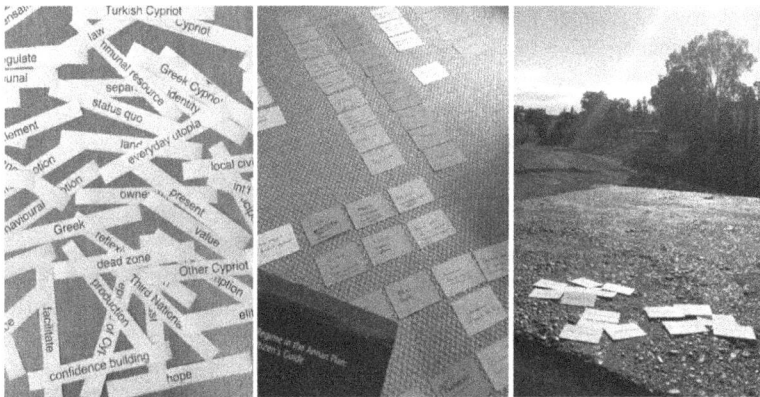

Figure 5.9 Converting text into mobile objects so that they can interact with each other and with the wider world. Images: Amanda Perry-Kessaris.

This brief is designed to prompt and facilitate you to isolate and confront, first, key concepts, events, relations and actors in your research, and then whole arguments, so that you can see them in relation to each other and in relation to key locations.

Process

Watch 'Actor Network Theory in Plain English', a film by Spreadlove (2009) available via YouTube.

Return to your Research Proposition (Brief 2). Identify all the key elements—for example, concepts, events, actors.

- Cut or tear several sheets of blank A4 into eight rectangles ('cards').
- In thick black pen write on each card one element—concept, location, event, actor etc.
- Experiment with organizing the cards using different criteria—for example, organize them according to the type of element, by time, scale or scope, at random. What is the effect of thinking in terms of each of these different criteria? With multiple criteria? Which criteria seem most important and why?
- Experiment with organizing the cards in different layouts—for example, stack them, run them horizontally or vertically.

Now experiment with telling the story that is at the heart of your research using the cards:

- Record yourself and watch/listen back.
- Consider: What has been revealed in this process. For example, has it perhaps overwritten, reinforced or revealed your prior narrative?[9]

Extension: Substitute images for words and repeat.

Brief 15: Observation

This brief is designed to prompt and facilitate you to look closely so that you are more likely to notice and capture information in the world around you that is relevant to your research, including by drawing. Whether or not you think you are any good at it, drawing is an effective 'means to *attune ourselves*' to the world, including that which we wish to research and perhaps influence. For example, ethnographers use drawing 'as a form of observation'—they 'dra[w] to see' (Woodward 2020, 139, and 253. Quoting Andrew Causey).

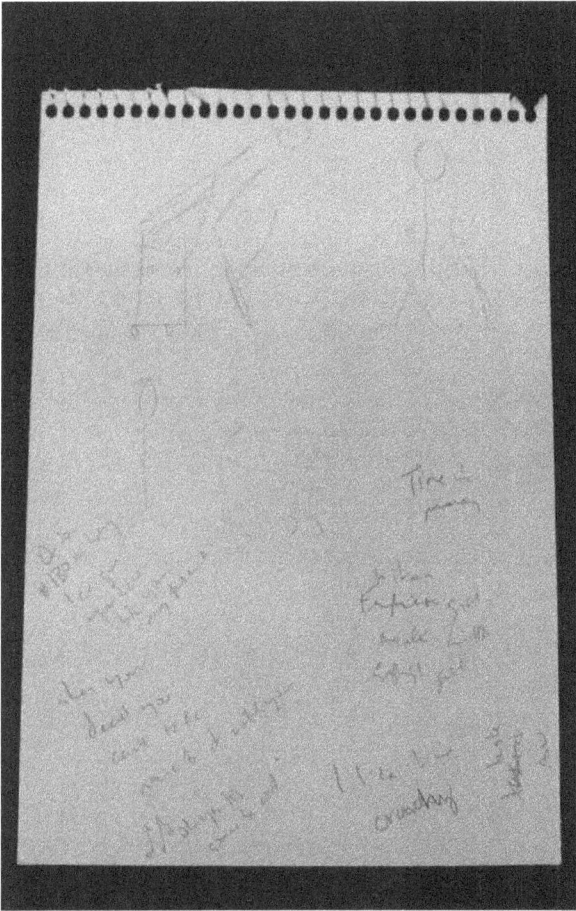

Figure 5.10 Documenting observed posture and conversation snippets in Ridley Road street market as part of the EXCHANGE (see further in Perry-Kessaris 2017i). Images: Amanda Perry-Kessaris.

Process

Watch 'The Girl with the Chewing Gum', a film by John Smith (1976) available via YouTube.

Identify a zoo that hosts live CCTV footage of an animal that interests you.

•   Watch the live stream for at least 30 minutes. Make notes detailing the setting and the action and sketch a moment that strikes you as particularly interesting.

- Consider: If you were able to speak to the animal, what questions would you ask it? What would you do with the answers?

Identify a geographical area that is somehow connected to your research, or to you as a researcher. 'Visit' it using Google maps. It may be a location that you know well or not at all.

- View the location in 'map' mode. Zoom in and out and explore the edges of your screen.
- Make notes detailing what you can see. Consider: How 'busy' is the scene—how many points of interest, roads, waterways, transport hubs? What patterns are made by natural and manmade features? Sketch one.
- View the map in 'satellite' mode. What is visible in this view that was not before? Zoom in and out.
- Consider: Which of your research sub-questions (see Brief 1 Outlining and Brief 2 Proposing) might this process help to answer?

Visit a public place and repeat the process, this time observing humans.

- In what ways are you, the observer, shaping what is being observed?
- If you were able to speak to the people you were observing, what questions would you ask them?
- What freedoms and constraints does observation bring to you as a researcher?

Notes

1 For 100 examples of learning research methods by doing beyond design and beyond law, see Dawson (2016).
2 This brief is adapted from an exercise proposed by Charles Debattista at the University of Southampton.
3 For example, the labyrinth was introduced to the University of Kent campus in 2008 as a quiet space, a teaching and learning space and an art installation. In addition to the full-scale labyrinth with sweeping views, it includes several benches with finger labyrinths carved into them. These can offer greater privacy and may also be more accessible to those whose vision is impaired.
4 This brief is adapted from an exercise proposed by Paul Bailey at the London College of Communication.
5 This brief is adapted from an exercise proposed by Bryony Quinn at the London College of Communication.
6 Note that the calliper introduced in the video might be treated as an object in the sense that it is part of a collection, but I chose to set that aside and to treat it as a thing.

7 See further in MacGregor (2012) and Hannan and Longair (2017).
8 For a general introduction to visualizing data, see Tufte (1990). For specific advice on how to visualize quantitative and qualitative data, including how to access free software, see Kirk (2019) and the Visualising Data website.
9 For more on storyboarding as an analytical tool, see Ayrton (2020); for more on storyboarding at any stage in the research process, see Dunleavy (2014).

Bibliography

ABC (2021) 'Stuff the British stole'. Podcast. https://www.abc.net.au/radionational/programs/stuff-the-british-stole/

Adler, M (2007) *Recognising the Problem: Socio-Legal Research Training in the UK.* London: Nuffield Foundation.

Advance HE (2019a) *Equality + Higher Education Staff Statistical Report 2019.* York: Advance HE.

Advance HE (2019b) *Equality + Higher Education Students Statistical Report 2019.* York: Advance HE.

Agamben, G and Fort, J (2007) 'In praise of profanation' 10 *Log* 23–32.

Ahmed, S (2012) *On Being Included: Racism and Diversity in Institutional Life.* London: Duke University Press.

Ahmed, S (2019) *What's the Use: On the Uses of Use.* London: Duke University Press.

Ahmed, S (2020) *What's the Use: On the Uses of Use.* Durham, NC: Duke University Press.

Akama, Y Pink, S and Sumartojo, S (2018) *Uncertainty and Possibility: New Approaches to Future Making in Design Anthropology.* London: Bloomsbury Academic Press.

Allbon, E (2018) 'Seeing law with new eyes: The legal design sprint' *LawBore* 1 August 2018. https://blog.lawbore.net/2018/08/seeing-law-with-new-eyes-the-legal-design-sprint/amandaperrykessaris.org

Antaki, M (2012) 'The turn to imagination in legal theory: The re-enchantment of the world?' 23 *Law Critique* 1–20.

ArtAngel (n.d.) website. Available at https://www.artangel.org.uk/in-the-shadow-of-the-state/the-touching-contract/

Asad, M (2019a) 'Prefigurative design as a method for research justice' 3:CSCW *Proceedings of the ACM on Human-Computer Interaction* Article 41 (November 2019) 18 pages.

Asad, M (2019b) *Sculpting Reality from Our Dreams: Prefigurative Design for Civic Engagement.* Dissertation. Georgia Institute of Technology, Atlanta.

Askeland, B (2020) 'The potential of abductive legal reasoning' 33:1 *Ratio Juris* 66–81.

Ausburn L and Ausburn F (1978) 'Visual literacy: Background, theory and practice' 15:4 *Programmed Learning and Educational Technology* 291–297.

Avgerinou, M and Ericson, J (1997) 'A review of the concept of Visual Literacy' 28:4 *British Journal of Educational Technology* 280–291.

Ayrton (2020) 'The case for creative, visual and multimodal methods in operationalising concepts in research design: An examination of storyboarding trust stories' *The Sociological Review* 1–21.

Baines, P and Haslam, A (2012) *Type and Typography*. London: Laurence King Publishing.

Banakar, R and Travers, M eds. (2005) *Theory and Method in Sociolegal Research*. Oxford: Hart.

Banerjee, A and Duflo, E (2010) *Poor Economics*. London: Penguin.

Barton, G and James, A (2017) 'Threshold concepts, LEGO® SERIOUS PLAY® and whole systems thinking: Towards a combined methodology' 12:2 *Practice and Evidence of Scholarship of Teaching and Learning in Higher Education* 249–271.

Bason, C (2014) *Design for Policy*. London: Routledge.

Bayazit, N (2004) 'Investigating design: A review of forty years of design research. 20:1 *Design Issues* 16–29.

BBC (2010) 'History of the world in 100 objects'. Podcast. https://www.bbc.co.uk/programmes/b00nrtd2/episodes/downloads

BBC Radio Four (2017–2020) 'The fix' https://www.bbc.co.uk/programmes/b0925737

Bennett, J (2010) *Vibrant Matter*. Durham, NC: Duke University Press.

Bennett, C L and Rosner, D K (2019) 'The promise of empathy: Design, disability, and knowing the "other"' in CHI 2019, 4–9 May 2019, Glasgow, Scotland, UK.

Berger, J (1972) *Ways of Seeing*. London: Penguin.

Bergold, J and Thomas, S (2012) 'Participatory research methods: A methodological approach in motion' 13(1) *Forum: Qualitative Social Research* Art 30.

Boehnert, J and Onafuwa, D (2016) 'Design as symbolic violence: Reproducing the 'isms' + a framework for allies' in *Intersectional Perspectives on Design, Politics and Power School of Arts and Communication*. Malmö University, 14 and 15 November 2016. Malmo: Sweden.

Brown, B (2001) 'Thing theory' 28:1 *Critical Inquiry* 1–22.

Brown, T (2009) *Change by Design*. New York: Harper.

Browne, S (2016) 'The touching contract London (with Jesse Jones)'. https://www.sarahbrowne.info/work/the-touching-contract-london/

Browne, S and Jones, J (2016) 'The touching contract' *Film*. https://vimeo.com/218640566

Brunschwig, C R (2001) *Visualisierung von Rechtsnormen: Legal Design [Visualization of Legal Norms: Legal Design]*. Schulthess. Vol 45.

Brunschwig, C R (2019) 'Contract comics and the visualisation, audio-visualisation and multisensorialization of law' 46:2 *University of Western Australia Law Review* 191.

Bryman, A (2016) *Social Research Methods* 5th Edition. Oxford: Oxford University Press.

Buchanan, R (1985) 'Declaration by design/l rhetoric, argument and demonstration in design practice' II:1 *Design Issues* 4.

Buchanan, R (1992) 'Wicked problems in design thinking' 8:2 *Design Issues* 5–21.

Burns, C, Cottam, H, Vanstone, C and Winhall, J (2005) *Transformation Design* Red Paper 2. London: Design Council.

Business and Human Rights Resource Centre Kik Lawsuit (re Pakistan) website. https://www.business-humanrights.org/en/latest-news/kik-lawsuit-re-pakistan/

Butler, J (1993) *Bodies that Matter: On the Discursive Limits of 'Sex'*. London: Routledge.

Candlin, F and Guins, R eds. (2009) 'Introducing objects' in *The Object Reader*. London: Routledge.

Candy, S (2021) 'Adding dimensions to development futures with UNDP' *The Futuryst* 31 March 2021. https://futuryst.blogspot.com/2021/03/experiential -futures-undp.html

Castoriadis, C (1975) *L'institution imaginaire de la societé* Paris: Editions du Seuil.

CCCI/KKTO Cyprus Chambers of Commerce and Industry and Turkish Cypriot Chamber of Commerce (2011) 'The Nine-O'Clock News in the Year 2030' *Video*. https://youtu.be/Pbrk1i4xXBI

Charman, H (2010) 'Designerly learning: Workshops for schools at the Design Museum' 15:30 *Design and Technology Education: An International Journal* 28.

Chilisa B (2012) *Indigenous Research Methods*. Thousand Oaks, CA: Sage.

Cooper, D (2017) 'Prefiguring the state' 49:2 *Antipode* 335.

Cooper, D (2020) 'Towards an adventurous institutional politics: The prefigurative 'as if' and the reposing of what's real' 68:5 *The Sociological Review* 893–916.

Corsín Jiménez, A (2014) 'Introduction: The prototype: More than many and less than one' 7:4 *Journal of Cultural Economy* 381–398.

Cottam, H (2018) *Radical Help: How We Can Remake the Relationships between us and Revolutionise the Welfare State*. London: Virago.

Cotterrell, R (1998) 'Why must legal ideas be interpreted sociologically?' 25:2 *Journal of Law and Society* 171–192.

Cotterrell, R (2002) 'Seeking similarity, appreciating difference: comparative law and communities' in A Harding and E Örücü eds. *Comparative Law in the 21st Century*. London: Kluwer Law International. 35–54.

Cotterrell, R (2006) *Law, Culture and Society: Legal Ideas in the Mirror of Social Theory*. Aldershot: Ashgate.

Cotterrell, R (2018) *Sociological Jurisprudence: Juristic thought and Social Inquiry*. London: Routledge.

Creutzfeldt, N, Mason, M and McConnachie, K eds. (2019). *Routledge Handbook of Socio Legal Theory and Methods*. London: Routledge.

Criado Perez, C (2020) *Invisible Women: Exposing Data Bias in a World Designed for Men*. New York: Vintage.

Cross, N (2001) 'Designerly ways of knowing: Design discipline versus design science' 17:3 *Design Issues* 49.

Crow, D (2003) *Visible Signs*. London: AVA Publishing.

d.school (n.d.) 'A virtual crash course in design thinking' https://dschool.stanford. edu/resources-collections/a-virtual-crash-course-in-design-thinking

Darian-Smith, E (2013) *Laws and Societies in Global Contexts: Contemporary Approaches*. Cambridge: Cambridge University Press.

Davies, M (2017) *Law Unlimited*. London: Routledge.

Davies, S (2018) 'Characterizing hacking: Mundane engagement in US hacker and makerspaces' 43:2 *Science, Technology and Human Values* 171–197.

Dawson, C (2016) *100 Activities for Teaching Research Methods.* London: Sage.

Design Council (2015) *The Design Process: What is the Double Diamond?* http://www.designcouncil.org.uk/news-opinion/design-process-what-double-diamond

Design Council (2017) *Designing a Future Economy: Developing Design Skills for Productivity and Innovation.* London: Design Council.

Design Council (2018) *The Design Economy 2018: The State of Design in the UK.* London: Design Council.

Development Impact and You website https://diytoolkit.org

DiSalvo, C (2012) *Adversarial Design.* London: MIT Press.

DiSalvo, C (2016) 'Design and prefigurative politics' 8:1 *The Journal of Design Strategies* 29–35.

Dorst, K (2015) *Frame Innovation: Create New Thinking by Design.* London: MIT Press.

Dorst, K, Kaldor, L, Klippan, L and Watson, R (2016) *Designing for the Common Good.* Amsterdam: BIS Publishers.

Dunleavy, P (2014) 'Storyboarding research' *Writing for Research* 18 August 2014. https://medium.com/advice-and-help-in-authoring-a-phd-or-non-fiction/storyboarding-research-b430cebd5ccd

Dunne, A (1998). *Hertzian Tales: Electronic Products, Aesthetic Experience and Critical Design.* London: Royal College of Art Computer Related Design Research Publications, p. 39.

Dunne, A and Raby, F (2013) *Speculative Everything: Design, Fiction, and Social Dreaming.* London: MIT Press.

Eames, R and Eames C (1977) 'Powers of ten'. Available at: https://www.eamesoffice.com/the-work/powers-of-ten/

Elam, K (2004) *Grid Systems: Principles of Organising Type.* New York: Princeton Architectural Press.

Elam, K (2007) *Typographic Systems.* New York: Princeton Architectural Press.

Enright, M and Kinsella, T (2021) 'Legal aesthetics in *the touching contract*: Memory, exposure and transformation' *Law, Culture and Humanities* 1–23. DOI: 10.1177/1743872120987113.

Escobar, A (2017) *Designs for the Pluriverse: Radical Interdependence, Autonomy and the Making of Worlds.* Durham, NC: Duke University Press.

Fast Track Impact website https://www.fasttrackimpact.com

Forensic Architecture website https://forensic-architecture.org

Fougère, M and Meriläinen, E (2021) 'Exposing three dark sides of social innovation through critical perspectives on resilience' 28:1 *Industry and Innovation* 1–18.

Four Legs Good (2018) https://compassliveart.org.uk//festival/events/four-legs-good

Frayling, C (1993) 'Research in art and design' 1:1 *Royal College of Art Research Papers* 1.

Fry, T (2017) 'Design for/by "The Global South"' 15:1 *Design Philosophy Papers* 3–37.

Gaver, B, Dunne, T and Pacenti, E. (1999) 'Cultural probes' 6:1 *Interactions* 21–29.

Genn, H, Partington, M and Wheeler, S (2006) *The Nuffield Inquiry on Empirical Legal Research*. London: Nuffield Foundation.

Giddens, A (1990) *The Consequences of Modernity*. Stanford, CA: Stanford University Press.

Giddens, T ed. (2015) *Graphic Justice: Intersections of Comics and Law*. London: Routledge.

Goodrich, P (2015) *Legal Emblems and Art of Law: Obiter Depicta as the Vision of Governance*. New York: Cambridge University Press.

Gulliksen, M S, Dishke-Hondzel, C, Härkki, T and Seitamaa-Hakkarainen, P (2016) 'Embodied making and design learning' 9:1 *Form Akademisk* Special Issue from Learn X Design-conference DRS/CUMULUS, Chicago 2015. 1–5.

Haapio, H and Passera, S (2013) 'Visual law: What lawyers need to learn from information designers' *Voxpopulii* 15 May 2013. http://blog.law.cornell.edu/voxpop/2013/05/15/visual-law-what-lawyers-need-to-learn-from-information-designers/

Hagan, M (n.d.) *Law by Design*. Available at: http://www.lawbydesign.co/en/home/

Hagan, M (2017) 'Community testing traffic court prototypes' *Legal Design Lab* 15 December 2017. https://www.legaltechdesign.com/2017/12/community-testing-traffic-court-prototypes/

Hammersley, M (2016) Review. 'Iddo Tavory and Stefan Timmermans, *abductive analysis*: *Theorizing qualitative research*' 16:6 *Qualitative Research* 748–750.

Hammersley, M and Atkinson, P (2007) *Ethnography: Principles into Practice*. London: Routledge.

Hannan, L and Longair, A (2017) *History through Material Culture*. Manchester: Manchester University Press.

Hatay, M, Mullen, F and Kalimeri, J (2008) *Intra-Island Trade in Cyprus: Obstacles, Oppositions and Psychological Barriers* PCC paper 2/2008. Nicosia: Prio Cyprus Centre.

Hockings, C (2010) 'Inclusive learning and teaching in higher education: A synthesis of research' Advance HE. https://www.advance-he.ac.uk/knowledge-hub/inclusive-learning-and-teaching-higher-education-synthesis-research

Hohman, J and Joyce, D (2017) *Objects of International Law*. Oxford: Oxford University Press.

Home for Cooperation website http://www.home4cooperation.info

Hunter, R, McGlynn, C and Rackley, E (2010) *Feminist Judgements: From Theory to Practice*. Oxford: Hart.

Huppatz, D J (2015) 'Revisiting Herbert Simon's "science of design"' 31:2 *Design Issues* 29.

Hustwit, G (2007) 'Helvetica' *Documentary*. https://www.hustwit.com/helvetica.

IDEO (2009) *Field Guide to Human-Centred Design*. London.

In the Shadow of the State website https://www.artangel.org.uk/project/in-the-shadow-of-the-state/

Ingold, T (2010) 'Bringing things to life: Creative entanglements in a World of materials' Working Paper 15 NCRM Working Paper Series.

Ingold, T (2013) *Making: Anthropology, Archaeology, Art and Architecture*. London: Routledge.

Institute of Making website https://www.instituteofmaking.org.uk/

Irani, L (2018) '"Design thinking": Defending Silicon Valley at the apex of global labor hierarchies' 4 *Catalyst: Feminism, Theory, Technoscience* 1 (May 2018).

Jacob M-A (2017) The strikethrough: An approach to regulatory writing and professional discipline 37:1 *Legal Studies* 137–161.

Jacob, M-A and Macdonald, A (2019) 'A change of heart: Retraction and body' 15 *Law Text Culture* 262–275.

James, A and Brookfield, S D (2014) *Engaging Imagination: Helping Students Become Creative and Reflective Thinkers*. Hoboken, NJ: Jossey-Bass.

Johns, F (2019) 'From planning to prototypes: New ways of seeing like a State' 82:5 *Modern Law Review* 833–863.

Julier, G (2017) *Economies of Design*. London: Sage.

Julier, G and Kimbell, L (2016) *Co-Producing Social Futures through Design Research*. Brighton: University of Brighton.

Kafer, A (2013) *Feminist, Queer, Crip*. Bloomington, IN: Indiana University Press.

Kane, J (2013) *A Type Primer*. London: Lawrence King Publishing.

Kane, P (2004) *The Play Ethic: A Manifesto for a Different Way of Living*. New York: Macmillan.

Kang, H J and Kendall, S (2019) 'Legal materiality' in Stern, S. Del Mar, M. and Meyler, B. eds. *The Oxford Handbook of Law and Humanities*. Oxford: Oxford University Press.

Kara, H (2015) *Creative Research Methods in the Social Sciences: A Practical Guide*. Bristol: Policy Press.

Kara, H (2018) *Research Ethics in the Real World: Euro-Western and Indigenous Perspectives*. Bristol: Policy Press.

Karana, A, Hekkert, P and Kandachar, P (2010) 'A tool for meaning driven materials selection' 31 *Materials and Design* 2932–2941.

Kieft, E (2020) Embodied methodologies: The body as research instrument. National Centre for Research Methods online learning resource. Available at: https://www.ncrm.ac.uk/resources/online/embodied_methodologies/ (Accessed 21 November 2020).

Kimbell, L (2011) 'Rethinking design thinking: Part I' 3:3 *Design and Culture* 285–306

Kimbell, L (2012) 'Rethinking design thinking: Part II' 4:2 *Design and Culture* 129–148.

Kimbell, L (2015) *Applying Design Approaches to Policy Making: Discovering PolicyLab*. Brighton: Brighton University.

Kimbell, L (2019) 'Designing policy objects: Anti-heroic design' in Gamman, L. and Fisher, T. eds. *Tricky Design*. London: Bloomsbury.

Kimbell, L and Bailey, J (2017) 'Prototyping and the new spirit of policy-making' 13:3 *CoDesign* 214–226, DOI: 10.1080/15710882.2017.1355003

Kimbell, L and Vesnić-Alujević, L (2020) 'After the toolkit: Anticipatory logics and the future of government' 3:2 *Policy Design and Practice* 95–108.

Kirk, A (2019) *Data Visualisation: A Handbook on Data-Driven Design*. Los Angeles, CA: Sage.

Klein, J T (1996) *Crossing Boundaries: Knowledge, Disciplinarities and Interdisciplinarities*. London: University Press of Virginia.

Knapp, J, Zeratsky, J and Kowitzt, B (2016) *Sprint: How to Solve Big Problems and Test New Ideas in Just Five Days*. New York: Bantam Press.

Kovács, G and Spens, K M (2005) 'Abductive reasoning in logistics research' 35:2 *International Journal of Physical Distribution & Logistics Management* 132–144.

Kritzner, H M (2009) 'Research is a messy business: An archaeology of the craft of socio-legal research' in Halliday, A and Schmidt, P eds. *Conducting Law and Society Research: Reflections on Methods and Practices*. New York: Cambridge University Press.

Labyrinth Society website https://labyrinthsociety.org

Labyrinths in Britain website https://labyrinthsinbritain.uk

Lakoff, G and Johnson, M (1980) *The Metaphors We Live By*. Chicago, IL: University of Chicago Press.

Latour, B (2002) 'What is iconoclash? Or Is there a world beyond the image wars?' in Weibel, P and Latour, B eds. *Iconoclash, Beyond the Image-Wars in Science, Religion and Art*. ZKM and MIT Press, 14–37.

Latour, B (2009) *The Making of Law: An Ethnography of the Conseil d'Etat*. London: Polity Press.

Law, J (2004) *After Method: Mess in Social Research*. London: Routledge.

Laws, J (2016) 'Interview: With Sarah Browne and Jesse Jones; "Towards a Post-Patriarchal State"' *Visual Artist's News Sheet*, Nov/Dec 2016.

Lim, Y, Stolterman, E and Tenengerg, J (2008) 'The anatomy of prototypes: Prototypes as filters, prototypes as manifestations of design ideas' 15:2 *ACM Transactions on Computer Interaction* Article 7.

Lorde, A (1984). *Sister Outsider: Essays and Speeches*. Trumansburg, NY: Crossing Press.

Lupton, E (2010) *Thinking with Type*. New York: Princeton Architectural Press.

Lupton, E ed. (2011) *Graphic Design Thinking: Beyond Brainstorming*. New York: Princeton Architectural Press.

Lyon, D and Cabarelli, G (2016) 'Researching young people's orientations to the future: The methodological challenges of using arts practice' 16:4 *Qualitative Research* 430–445.

MacGregor, N (2012) *A History of the World in 100 Objects*. London: Penguin Books.

Maeckelbergh M (2011) 'Doing is believing: Prefiguration as strategic practice in the alterglobalization movement' 10:1 *Social Movement Studies* 1–20.

Malpass, M (2016) 'Critical design practice: Theoretical perspectives and methods of engagement 19:3 *The Design Journal* 473–489, pp. 475 and 478.

Malpass, M (2017) *Critical Design in Context: History, Theory, and Practices*. London: Bloomsbury.

Manderson, D (2019) *Danse Macabre: Temporalities of Law in the Visual Arts*. New York: Cambridge University Press.

Mannay, D (2016) *Visual, Narrative and Creative Research Methods: Application, Reflection and Ethics*. London: Routledge.

Manzini, E (2015) *Design, When Everybody Designs*. Cambridge, MA: MIT Press.

Mazé, R (2016) 'Design and the future: Temporal politics of making a difference' in Smith, R C, Vangkilde, K T Kjaersgaard, M G, Otto, T, Halse, J and Binder, T eds. *Design Anthropological Futures*. London: Bloomsbury Publishing.

Mazé, R and Redström, J (2007) 'Difficult forms: Critical practices of design and research' 1 *Research Design Journal* 28–39.

McCloskey, D (2002) *The Secret Sins of Economics*. Chicago, IL: Prickly Paradigm Press. Available at: http://www.prickly-paradigm.com/titles/secret -sins-economics

Mcdermont, M with the Productive Margins Collective (2018) 'Alternative imaginings of regulation: An experiment in co-production' 45:1 *Journal of Law and Society* 156.

McKeever, G and Royal-Dawson, L (2021) 'Using human centred design to break down barriers to legal participation' in Allbon, E and Perry-Kessaris, A eds. *Design and Visualisation in Legal Education: Access to the Law*. London: Routledge.

McNerney, L (2014) 'The craft of writing effectively' *Video of Lecture*. University of Chicago Social Sciences. Available at: https://youtu.be/vtIzMaLkCaM (Accessed 22 November 2020).

Memon, R A and Jivraj, S (2020) 'Trust, courage and silence: Carving out decolonial spaces in higher education through student–staff partnerships' 54:4 *The Law Teacher* 475–488.

Miller, H, Thebault-Spieker, J, Chang, S, Johnson, I, Terveen, L and Hecht, B (2016). '"blissfully happy" or "ready to fight": Varying interpretations of emoji' in Proceedings of the 10th International Conference on Web and Social Media, ICWSM 2016 (pp. 259–268) Cologne, Germany: AAAI Press.

Mindsets website https://mindsetsonline.co.uk

Moran, L (2015) 'Judicial pictures as legal life-writing data and a research method' 42:1 *Journal of Law and Society* 74–101.

Mulcahy, L (2011) *Legal Architecture: Justice, Due Process and the Place of Law*. London: Routledge.

Mulcahy, L (2017) 'Eyes of the law: A visual turn in socio-legal studies?' 44:1 *Journal of Law and Society* S111–S128.

Mulcahy, L and Rowden, E (2019) *The Democratic Courthouse: A Modern History of Design, Due Process and Dignity*. London: Routledge.

Murray, R, Caulier-Grice, J and Mulgan, G (2010) *The Open Book of Social Innovation*. Young Foundation/NESTA, March 2010. London.

National Public Radio (NPR) (2013a) 'Planet money makes a t-shirt and follows its global journey'. Podcast. https://www.npr.org/series/262481306/planet-money-t -shirt-project-series

National Public Radio (NPR) (2013b) 'Planet money makes a t-shirt: The world behind a simple shirt, in five chapters'. *Visuals*. https://apps.npr.org/tshirt/#/title

Navaro-Yashin, Y (2012) *The Make-Believe Space: Affective Geography in a Postwar Polity*. Durham, NC: Duke University Press.

Newman, D (n.d.) The design squiggle. https://thedesignsquiggle.com

Nind, M and Lewthwaite, S (2019) 'A conceptual-empirical typology of social science research methods pedagogy' *Research Papers in Education*. 35(4), 1470–1146.

Norman, D [(1988] 2013) *The Design of Everyday Things*. Cambridge, MA: MIT Press.

Norman, D (2004) *Emotional Design*. Basic Books.

Norman, D (2010) 'Why design education must change' *Core77* November 26. New York. https://www.core77.com

Oswald, D (2012) 'The information department at the Ulm School of Design' in Farias, P L, Calvera, A Braga, M and Schincariol, Z eds. *Design Frontiers: Territories, Concepts, Technologies* ICDHS 2012 – 8th Conference of the International Committee for Design History & Design Studies. São Paulo: Blucher. DOI 10.5151/design-icdhs-011

Page Moreau, C and Gundersen Engeset, M (2016) 'The downstream consequences of problem-solving mindsets: How playing with LEGO influences creativity' 53:1 *Journal of Marketing Research* 18–30.

Pahuja, S (2021) 'Practical methodology: Writing about how we do research' in Deplano, R. and Tsagourias, N eds. *Handbook on Methodologies in International Law*. Cheltenham: Edward Elgar.

Papadakis, Y, Peristianis, N and Welz, G eds. (2006) *Divided Cyprus: Modernity, History and an Island in Conflict*. Bloomington, IN: Indiana University Press. New Anthropologies of Europe.

Pater, R (2013) *Drone Survival Guide*. Available at: http://www.dronesurvivalguide.org

Pater, R (2016) *The Politics of Design: A (not so) Global Manual for Visual Communication*. Amsterdam: BIS.

Pauwels, L (2010) 'Visual Sociology Reframed: An Analytical Synthesis and Discussion of Visual Methods in Social and Cultural Research' 38:4 *Sociological Methods and Research* 545–581.

Pauwels, L (2011) 'An Integrated Conceptual Framework for Visual Social Research' in Margolis, E and Pauwels, L eds. *The Sage Handbook of Visual Research Methods*. London: Sage, pp. 3–23.

Peabody, M A and Noyes, S (2017) 'Reflective boot camp: Adapting LEGO® SERIOUS PLAY® in higher education' 18:2 *Reflective Practice* 232–243.

Peirce, C S ([1878] 1992) 'Deduction, Induction and Hypothesis' in N. Houser and Kloesel, C. ed. *The Essential Pierce*: *Selected Philosophical Writings* Vol 1 (1876–1893). Bloomington and Indianapolis, IN: Indian University Press, pp. 186–199.

Peirce, C S ([1903] 1998) 'Pragmatism as the Logic of Abduction (Lecture VII)' in The Pierce Edition Project ed. *The Essential Pierce*: *Selected Philosophical Writings (1893–1913)*. Bloomington and Indianapolis, IN: Indian University Press, pp. 229–240.

Perry, J (2019) *Connecting on Hate Crime Data in England and Wales*. Brussels: CEJI.

Perry-Kessaris, A (2008) *Global Business Local Law: The Indian Legal System as a Communal Resource in Investment Relations*. Aldershot: Ashgate.

Perry-Kessaris, A (2015) 'Approaching the econo-socio-legal' 11:16 *Annual Review of Law & Social Science* 1–18.

Perry-Kessaris, A (2014a) 'The case for a visualized economic sociology of legal development' 67 *Current Legal Problems* 169–198.

Perry-Kessaris, A (2014b) 'What can graphic design reveal about law?' *Film.* https://vimeo.com/manage/videos/112165899

Perry-Kessaris, A (2016a) 'EXCHANGE' *Approaching Law* 17 February 2016. https://amandaperrykessaris.org/2016/02/17/exchange/

Perry-Kessaris, A (2016b) 'Exploring the potential of materials to "fire imagination" and "advance conceptualisation"' *Approaching Law* 10 August 2016. https://amandaperrykessaris.org/2016/08/10/exploring-the-potential-of-materials-to-fire-imagination-and-advance-conceptualisation/

Perry-Kessaris, A (2016c) 'Sociolegal model-making 4: Discussion' *Approaching Law* 22 September 2016. https://amandaperrykessaris.org/2016/09/22/mass-sociolegal-visualisation/

Perry-Kessaris, A (2016d) 'Sociolegal model making 5: Material metaphoricization' *Approaching Law* 31 October 2016. https://amandaperrykessaris.org/2016/10/31/sociolegal-model-making-5-material-metaphorization/

Perry-Kessaris A (2016e) 'Sociolegal model-making 6: Place-holding' *Approaching Law* 19 December 2016. https://amandaperrykessaris.org/2016/12/19/socio-legal-model-making-6-place-holding/

Perry-Kessaris A. (2017a) 'The pop-up museum of legal objects project: An experiment in "sociolegal design"' 68:3 *Northern Ireland Legal Quarterly* Special Issue on the Pop-up Museum of Legal Objects 225–244.

Perry-Kessaris A (2017b) 'The re-co-construction of legitimacy of/through the doing business indicators' 13:4 *International Journal of Law in Context* Special Issue on Global Social Indicators: Constructing Transnational Legitimacy 498–511.

Perry-Kessaris, A (2019) 'Legal design for practice, activism, policy and research' 46:2 *Journal of Law and Society* 185–210.

Perry-Kessaris, A (2020) 'Making sociolegal research more social by design: Anglo-German roots, rewards and risks' 21:6 *German Law Journal* 1427–1445.

Perry-Kessaris, A and Perry, J (2020) 'Enhancing participatory strategies with designerly ways for sociolegal impact: Lessons from research aimed at making hate crime visible in Europe' *Social and Legal Studies*. 835–857.

Perry-Kessaris, A and Renmei, A (2016) 'Materials-based gaze: An interview with Zoe Laughlin' *Video.* https://vimeo.com/190913526

Philippopoulos-Mihalopoulos, A. (2016) 'Flesh of the law: Material legal metaphors' 43:1 *Journal of Law and Society* 45–65.

Pink, S (2011) 'Drawing with our feet (and trampling the maps): Walking with video as a graphic anthropology' in T Ingold ed. *Redrawing Anthropology* 143-56. Farnham: Ashgate.

Policy Lab (2016) *Open Policy Making Toolkit.* https://www.gov.uk/guidance/open-policy-making-toolkit

Pritchard, T (2010) 'Typographic Hierarchy' *Film.* https://vimeo.com/13418563

Prown, J D (1982) 'Mind in matter: An introduction to material culture theory and method' 17:1 *Winterthur Portfolio* 1–19.

Pruitt, J and Grudin, J (2003) 'Personas: Practice and theory' in Proceedings of the Conference on Designing for User Experiences https://www.microsoft.com /en-us/research/wp-content/uploads/2017/01/personas-practice-and-theory.pdf (Accessed 18 December 2020).

Rado, D (n.d.) 'How to save yourself hours by using outline view properly' Available at: https://wordmvp.com/FAQs/Formatting/UsingOLView.htm

Ranjan, S (n.d.) 'Interview with artist Jack Tan' *Art/Law Networks*. Available at: https://artlawnetwork.org/interview-with-artist-jack-tan/

Raworth, K (2017) *Doughnut Economics*. London: Random House Business Books.

Raworth, R (2017) *Doughnut Economics: Seven Ways to Think Like a 21st-Century Economist*. London: Random House.

Reed, M (2018) *The Research Impact Handbook*. Fast Track Impact. https://www. fasttrackimpact.com/team.

Resnick, J and Curtis, D E (2011) *Representing Justice: The Creation and Fragility of Courts in Democracies: Invention, Controversy, and Rights in City-States and Democratic Courtrooms*. New Haven, CT: Yale University Press.

Rhinow, H, Koppen, E and Meinel, C (2012) 'Prototypes as boundary objects in innovation processes' Conference paper in the Proceedings of the 2012 International Conference on Design Research Society (DRS 2012), Bangkok, Thailand, July 2012.

Rittel, H W J and Weber, M M (1973) 'Dilemmas in a general theory of planning' 4:2 *Policy Sciences* 155–169.

Roberts, L E and Thrift, J (2002) *The Designer and the Grid*. Hove: Rotovision.

Robinson, R (2019) 'A portable paradise' in *Portable Paradise*. Leeds: Peepal Tree Press.

Rodrik, D (2016) *Economic Rules: Why Economics Works, When It Fails and How to Tell the Difference*. Oxford: Oxford University Press.

Rogers, N and Maloney, M eds. (2017) *Law as if Earth Really Mattered: The Wild Law Judgment Project*. London: Routledge.

Rose, G (2016) *Visual Methodologies: An Introduction to Researching with Visual Materials* 4th Edition. Oxford: Sage.

Said, E (1994) *Representations of the Intellectual*. New York: Vintage.

Saletnik, J (2007) 'Josef Albers, Eva Hesse, and the imperative of teaching' *Tate Papers* Spring 2007.

Sandhar, J and Omony, G (2019) '"I am free from the conflict, but I do not feel free": The experiences of child soldiers in Northern Uganda'. https://www.bri stol.ac.uk/media-library/sites/law/documents/new-sites-publications/Childso ldier%20comic.pdf

Saval, N (2019) 'How Bauhaus redefined what design could do for society' 4 February 2019 *New York Times Style Magazine*. Available at: https://www .nytimes.com/2019/02/04/t-magazine/bauhaus-school-architecture-history .html

Schwab, K (2018) 'Ideo breaks its silence on design thinking's critics' *FastCompany*. https://www.fastcompany.com/90257718/ideo-breaks-its-silence-on-design-thin kings-critics

Sherwin, R K (2011) *Vizualising Law in the Age of the Digital Baroque: Arabesques and Entanglements*. London: Routledge.

Simon, H A ([1969] 1996) *The Sciences of the Artificial* 3rd Edition. Cambridge, MA: MIT Press.

Simon, H A (1973) 'The structures of ill-structured problems' 4 *Artificial Intelligence* 181–201.

Smith, J (1976) 'The girl with the chewing gum' *Film*. https://youtu.be/57hJn -nkKSA

Social Accountability International SA8000 Guidelines website https://sa-intl.org/ programs/sa8000/

Socio-Legal Studies Association (SLSA) (2009) 'Statement of principles of ethical research practice 2001, revised in 2009'. https://www.slsa.ac.uk/index.php/ethic s-statement

Sode, Y (2019) 'Untitled. Poem commissioned for 'displays of power: A natural history of empire' Grant Museum of Zoology, September 2019 – March 2020. https://youtu.be/PWGD1SgyiNA

Solanke, Y (2017) 'Black female professors in the UK' *Runnymede Trust*. https:// www.runnymedetrust.org/blog/black-female-professors-in-the-uk

Spreadlove (2009) 'Actor Network Theory in Plain English' *Film*. https://youtu.be /X2YYxS6D-mI

St Clair, K (2016) *The Secret Lives of Colour*. London: John Murray Publishers.

Star, S L (1989) 'The structure of Ill-structured solutions: Boundary objects and heterogeneous distributed problem solving' in Huhs, M and Gasser, L eds. *Readings in Distributed Artificial Intelligence*. Menlo Park, CA: Morgan Kaufmann.

Star, S L and Griesemer, J R (1989) 'Institutional ecology, "translations" and boundary objects: Amateurs and professionals in Berkley's Museum of Vertebrate Zoology 1970–39' 19:3 *Social Studies of Science* 1–10.

Stickdorn, M, Lawrence, A, Hormness, M and Schenider, J (2018) *This is Service Design Doing*. Sebastopol, CA: O'Reilly Media.

Stratis, S ed. (2016) *Guide to Common Urban Imaginaries in Contested Spaces*. Berlin: Jovis.

Stylianou-Lambert, T and Bounia, A (2016) *The Political Museum*. London: Routledge.

Sudjic, D (2008) *The Language of Things*. London: Penguin.

Tan, J (2018) *Animal Justice Court Annual Review 2018*. Printed booklet. Self published.

Tan, J (2020a) 'Animal Justice Court R v Snoopy V&A Friday Late Jack Tan 2019'. *Video*. Available at: https://youtu.be/SkL65t_PKfo

Tan, J (2020b) 'Four legs good, two legs good' in Wagaine, S. *Vanishing Points: An Anthology of New Cultural Criticism*. Live Art Development Agency and Diverse Actions, pp. 23–28.

Tan, J website JackTan.net

Tavory, I and Timmermans, S (2014) *Abductive Analysis: Theorizing Qualitative Research*. Chicago, IL: Chicago University Press.

The Art/Law Network website https://artlawnetwork.org/

Tonkinwise, C (2014). 'Review of becoming human by design by Tony Fry (London/ New York: Berg, 2012)' 30:2 *Design Issues* 118–120.

Toolbox Toolbox https://www.toolboxtoolbox.com

Townsend, K and Burgess, J (2009) *Method in the Madness: Research Stories You Won't Read in Textbooks*. Oxford: Chandos.

Tufte, E R (1990) *Envisioning Information*. Cambridge, MA: Graphics Press.

Tuhiwai Smith, L (2012) *Decolonizing Methodologies: Research and indigenous peoples*. London: Zed Books.

TV 2 Danmark (2017) 'All that we share' *Video*. Available at: https://youtu.be/ jD8tjhVO1Tc

Tyler, P (2016) 'Defining your audience and managing complex projects' *Handling Ideas*. Available at: https://www.youtube.com/watch?v=pPfVoofkvl0 (Accessed: 17 October 2017).

UCL Department of Science and Technology Studies (2020) 'Untold narratives: Colonialism in natural history' *Video*. https://youtu.be/d8z8zovRTd4

UNDP (2016) *Innovation for 2030: UNDP Innovation Facility: 2015 Year in Review*. New York: UNDP.

Unger, U M (2021) *The Universal History of Legal Thought*. Deep Freedom Books.

University of Kent (2013) *The Labyrinth*. https://www.kent.ac.uk/creativecampus/ projects/learning/labyrinth/index.html

Van Der Veer Martens, B (2011) 'Approaching the Anti-collection' 59:4 *Library Trends* 568–587.

Vinsel, L (2017) 'Design thinking is kind of like syphilis: It's contagious and rots your brains' 6 December 2017. https://medium.com/@sts_news/design-thinking -is-kind-of-like-syphilis-its-contagious-and-rots-your-brains-842ed078af29

Vismann, C (2008) *Files: Law and Media Technology*. Palo Alto, CA: Stanford University Press.

Visualising Data website https://www.visualisingdata.com

Watkins, D, Lai-Chong L E, Barwick, J and Kirk, E (2018) 'Exploring children's understanding of law in their everyday lives' 38 *Legal Studies* 59–78.

Weingarden, L S (1985) 'Aesthetics politicized: William Morris to the Bauhaus' 38:3 *Journal of Architectural Education* 8–13.

Weizman, E (2017) *Forensic Architecture: Violence at the Threshold of Detectability*. New York: Zone Books.

Wenger, E (1998) *Communities of Practice: Learning, Meaning and Identity*. New York: Cambridge University Press.

Williams, C (n.d.) 'Mountains of metaphor' *Interactive Digital Game*. https://tldr.le gal/resource/mountains-of-metaphor.html

Williams, C (2019) *Beyond Embeddedness: Reshaping an Economic Sociology of Law*. PhD Thesis, SOAS University of London.

Willis, A-M (2006) 'Ontological designing: Laying the ground' 3 *Design Philosophy Papers Collection*. 80–98.

Willis, A-M (2015) 'Transition design: The need to refuse discipline and transcend instrumentalism' 13:1 *Design Philosophy Papers* 69–74.

Winhall, J (2019) 'Double diamond' *Design Council* September 16, 2019. https://me dium.com/design-council/double-diamond-jennie-winhall-59ebbe4a2ddb

Winter, S L (2007) 'Re-embodying Law' 58:3 *Mercer Law Review* 869.

Woodward, S (2020) *Material Methods: Researching and Thinking with Things.* London: Sage.

Woolf, V (1992 [1927]) 'A room of one's own' in *A Room of One's Own: Three Guineas.* Oxford: Oxford University Press.

World Bank (2015) *World Development Report 2015: Mind, Society, Knowledge and Behaviour.* Washington, DC: World Bank.

Yashaswi, P (2019) 'Indian designers dismiss "design-school propaganda" as they decolonise their work' *Dezeen.* 14 November 2019.

Zimmerman, J Forlizzi, J and Evenson, S (2007) 'Research through design as a method for interaction design research in HCI' *CHI 2007 Proceedings*, April 28–May 3, 2007, San Jose, CA.

Index

For Product Safety Concerns and Information please contact our EU
representative GPSR@taylorandfrancis.com
Taylor & Francis Verlag GmbH, Kaufingerstraße 24, 80331 München, Germany